GRAMMAR FOR WRITING 1
AN EDITING GUIDE TO WRITING

Joyce S. Cain

ALWAYS LEARNING

PEARSON

Grammar for Writing 1: An Editing Guide to Writing

Pearson ELT, 10 Bank Street, White Plains, NY 10606

Staff credits: The people who made up the *Grammar for Writing 1* team, representing editorial, production, design, and manufacturing are: Pietro Alongi, Rhea Banker, Christine Edmonds, Nancy Flaggman, Kathy Furgang, Jaime Lieber, Amy McCormick, Massimo Rubini, Paula Van Ells, and Marian Wassner.
Cover design: Barbara Perez
Text design: Barbara Perez
Text composition: ElectraGraphics, Inc.
Text font: ITC Stone Serif
Cover photo: John Elk/Getty Images

Library of Congress Cataloging-in-Publication Data
Cain, Joyce S.
  [Eye on editing]
  Grammar for writing 1 : an editing guide to writing/ Joyce S. Cain.
— 2nd ed.
      p. cm.
  Previously pub.: Eye on editing, 2001.
  Includes bibliographical references.
  ISBN 0-13-208898-3 — ISBN 0-13-208899-1 — ISBN 0-13-208900-9 1.
English language—Textbooks for foreign speakers. 2. English language—
Grammar—Problems, exercises, etc. 3. English language—Rhetoric—
Problems, exercises, etc. 4. Report writing—Problems, exercises, etc.
5. Editing—Problems, exercises, etc. I. Title. II. Title: Grammar for writing one.
  PE1128.C25 2012
  808'.02—dc22

                                                                2011008774

ISBN-10: 0-13-208898-3
ISBN-13: 978-0-13-208898-5

Printed in the United States of America

1 2 3 4 5 6 7 8 9 10—V011—16 15 14 13 12 11

Contents

To the Teacher

Grammar for Writing 1: An Editing Guide to Writing emphasizes the importance of the editing stage in the writing process. It is designed to meet the needs of ESL writers who have developed an intermediate level of fluency yet are unable to detect and correct grammatical errors in their writing. The concise grammatical explanations based on the most frequently occurring grammar errors of ESL students and the variety of editing exercises will help students begin to master the process of editing their own written work. *Grammar for Writing 1: An Editing Guide to Writing* can stand on its own or serve as a supplement to reading, writing, and grammar classes. It is also a useful reference guide for students.

The main goal of *Grammar for Writing 1: An Editing Guide to Writing* is to provide students with awareness to detect errors in their own writing and provide them with the tools to make necessary corrections. It aids students in the production of accurate, meaningful, and appropriate language. To this end, the grammar explanations and rules focus on those errors that are most prevalent in the writing of intermediate level students, although the book is an appropriate review for students at higher levels of writing proficiency as well.

Grammar for Writing 1: An Editing Guide to Writing is not intended to be a comprehensive grammar book. Grammar topics are based on an analysis of student writing errors. Because it focuses on specific problem areas, a cross-reference to three grammar books, *Basic English Grammar, Third Edition, Fundamentals of English Grammar, Fourth Edition,* and *Focus on Grammar 3, Fourth Edition,* has been provided to assist those who would like further grammatical explanations.

New to this Edition

A number of changes have been made in the second edition of *Grammar for Writing 1: An Editing Guide to Writing* based on feedback from teachers who use the book and from my own experiences using the book with students at both the university and community college levels.

- Two new chapters have been added: Sentence Structure and Punctuation and Commonly Confused Words. These new chapters replace the Verb Forms, Gerunds, and Infinitives and the Word Forms chapters, which have been moved to *Grammar for Writing 2: An Editing Guide to Writing.*

- A great effort was made to simplify the language and sentence complexity in this edition. This change allows community college students greater comprehension of the concepts and content in each chapter while still addressing the grammar and writing concepts needed by university writers. While the vocabulary has been simplified, it is based on the **Academic Word List**. Appendix 8 contains a list of vocabulary used in each chapter that comes from the Academic Word list.

- The Grammar Focus has been moved to the beginning of each chapter to trigger student knowledge of the chapter's grammar point before the Pretest is presented.

- Following the Pretest, Grammar In Context presents a short paragraph that contains multiple examples of the chapter's grammar concept. This paragraph has students tap into their passive awareness of the grammar concept—another opportunity for students to familiarize themselves with the concept before they are required to actively produce it.

- The Writing Topics section has been expanded to include a model student paragraph based on one of the writing topics that students are asked to write on. Students are instructed to notice the organization of the paragraph in addition to content that might help them as they begin to write their own paragraphs.

Although accurate editing remains the focus of *Grammar for Writing 1: An Editing Guide*, a greater emphasis is placed on writing in the second edition. Throughout the series, students work toward becoming independent writers who can plan, write, revise, and edit their work without relying on outside help.

Format and Content

Grammar for Writing 1: An Editing Guide is composed of twelve chapters. Eleven chapters focus on areas of grammar that are particularly problematic for ESL students, while the final chapter provides further practice. The first eleven chapters may be used in any order, and the final chapter may be drawn on as needed. It is possible to devote one week of class time to each chapter; however, depending on students' accuracy with each concept, there is enough material in the book when it is used as a supplemental text in a reading or writing class to fill a semester-long course.

Each of the first eleven chapters is composed of four sections. First, students develop an awareness of the grammar concept by reading a brief description, testing their prior knowledge with sentence-level items and noticing how the grammar point is used in a writing context. The following section includes grammar explanations. When explanations are broken into subtopics, each subtopic ends with a short, sentence-level Self Check, which enables students to verify their understanding of the subtopic before moving to the next. Charts and examples are used extensively to illustrate and visually reinforce the grammar points.

The exercises in the Editing Practice section focus on the task of editing discourse—a skill students need to apply in their own writing. The exercises move students from the sentence to the discourse level, and from more guided to less guided tasks. Exercise 1, like the Pretest, asks students to locate errors in sentence-level items. Exercises 2–4 provide paragraph-level editing practice based on adapted student writing. In Exercise 2, errors are pointed out for the student to correct; Exercise 3 generally requires students to supply the correct form of the given word; Exercise 4 asks students to locate and correct grammar errors in an unmarked piece of writing. Students are always told how many errors they must identify; however, just as in their own writing, they must scrutinize all sentences in order to edit the piece successfully. The exercises are appropriate for homework, in-class practice, or quizzes.

Each chapter ends with Writing Topics. Before students begin to write, they can read a sample paragraph based on one of the two guided writing tasks in the chapter. The sample paragraph not only models one of the writing topics but also provides students with an example of a paragraph with a topic sentence, supporting sentences, and a concluding sentence. Once students have studied the writing topic's expectations, they can easily move to writing their own paragraph and editing for the grammatical structures presented in the chapter. The writing topics, designed for paragraph writing, are based on themes that are accessible to all students without instruction on the content.

Chapter 12 consists of paragraph-level editing exercises that are similar to Exercise 4 in the earlier chapters. However, these paragraphs require students to edit for more than one type of grammar error at a time, providing them with further realistic practice.

The first appendix, Practice with Authentic Language, contains excerpts from published writing. In this exercise, students practice their editing skills by selecting the correct form from alternatives. The next four appendices offer students a reference guide to irregular verbs, spelling, capitalization, and punctuation, preposition use, and commonly used correction symbols. The editing log found in Appendix 6 asks students to record and correct their grammar mistakes in order to help them become aware of the errors they make most frequently. Appendix 7 is a grammar correlation between topics presented in *Grammar for Writing 1: An Editing Guide* and *Basic English Grammar, Third Edition, Fundamentals of English Grammar, Fourth Edition,* and *Focus on Grammar 3, Fourth Edition.* The final appendix is the Academic Word List.

Collaborative and Oral Activities

Grammar for Writing 1: An Editing Guide lends itself to individual work but is easily adapted to include more communicative activities. Suggestions for collaborative and oral activities include the following:

- After students take the Pretest, ask them to predict the grammar rules for the chapter.

- Have students work with a partner to read the paragraph following the Pretest. Together they can locate the target structures.

- Ask pairs of students to create editing exercises based on their own writing, focusing on the target structures.

- Ask students to submit samples of a target error from their own writing for the development of more exercises.

- Ask students to read their original paragraphs or exercises aloud to a partner to listen for grammatical correctness.

- Ask students to read their partner's writing aloud so that the writers can hear what they have written and check for errors.

- Ask a small group of students to develop a lesson about or an explanation of one grammar topic and present it to the class.

- Have partners, small groups, or the entire class discuss the sample paragraph in the Writing Topics section. Ask them to locate the topic sentence, major and minor supporting points, and concluding sentence.

- Have partners, small groups, or the entire class brainstorm on the writing topics, helping students develop ideas before they begin the writing assignment.

- Ask students to work collaboratively on the paragraph writing assignments and submit the collective group paragraph.

- Ask pairs or small groups to look at pieces of published writing and find examples of the target grammatical structures.

- Have a class discussion on the rhetorical features seen in the pieces of published writing in Appendix 1.

To the Student

Grammar for Writing 1: An Editing Guide presents the rules and practice you need to become a better writer and better editor of your writing. This book has a number of features that will help you accomplish these goals.

GRAMMAR TOPICS: The grammar topics in *Grammar for Writing 1: An Editing Guide* have been chosen based on an analysis of student writing. The errors you will focus on are ones that student writers make often and need to correct. Through practice, you will begin to find, correct, and eventually eliminate these common errors in your own writing.

BRIEF EXPLANATIONS: The brief, clear grammar explanations will help you focus on the key points that you need to edit your own work successfully. The charts and appendices provide handy tools for quick reference.

STUDENT WRITING: Most exercises are developed from student writing. Therefore, the exercises reflect topics and grammar points that are relevant to student writers.

SEQUENCE OF EXERCISES: The pretests help you assess your knowledge of each grammar topic and decide how much practice you need. The subsequent sample paragraphs and exercises in each chapter become progressively more difficult, allowing you to build skills and confidence as you work through the exercises. Finally, you are given the chance to produce and edit your own writing.

EXTRA EDITING: In general, when you edit your own writing, you will be looking for various types of errors, not just one type. Therefore, in Chapter 12, you will have additional practice editing for more than one error type in each exercise.

PUBLISHED WRITING: It is always helpful to notice how professional writers use the language. The Practice with Authentic Language exercises in Appendix 1 are drawn from published articles. They will allow you to become more aware of the structures used by professional writers in published material.

EDITING LOG: The editing log found in Appendix 6 will help you focus on the grammar errors that you make most frequently. By recording the grammar mistakes that your teacher finds in your paragraphs and essays, you will begin to see a pattern of certain errors. Once you know your grammar weaknesses, you can successfully edit for and eliminate them in future writing.

Acknowledgments

Many thanks to the students who have made *Grammar for Writing 1: An Editing Guide to Writing* possible, beginning with my former students at the University of California, Irvine and continuing with my current students at Fullerton College. It is their desire for accurate writing that has guided this book.

Many more thanks to the Pearson Longman editors and staff who have helped me navigate through the publishing process. I owe a great deal to Massimo Rubini, Paula Van Ells, Stacey Hunter, Kathy Furgang, and Marian Wassner, whose perceptive, accurate, and detailed suggestions have helped in the creation of this book. In addition, my colleagues at the University of California, Irvine and Fullerton College have been both helpful and supportive throughout this process. I thank them sincerely.

Finally, I want to thank my family, especially my husband, Paul, whose continued enthusiasm for this project has never wavered.

Expressing Present Time

GRAMMAR FOCUS

The three verb tenses discussed in this chapter—the simple present, the present progressive, and the present perfect—all express present time. However, the three tenses have different uses. Notice how they are used in the sentences below according to the time word that is chosen.

SIMPLE PRESENT	He **takes** six vitamins every day.
PRESENT PROGRESSIVE	We **are working** on a proposal right now.
PRESENT PERFECT	I **have driven** there many times.

Pretest

Check your understanding of the tenses that express present time. Put a check (✓) next to the sentences that are correct.

_____ **1.** I am loving classic English novels.

_____ **2.** Our professor is sick since Monday.

_____ **3.** My grandmother likes to tell me stories about her childhood. She still has remembered so much about her youth.

_____ **4.** My neighbor leaves for work at 7:30 every morning.

_____ **5.** Right now Pat has searched for information on the Internet.

_____ **6.** Mary and I have seen all of the old silent movies.

_____ **7.** Bob and Jack usually are working out at the gym five days a week.

_____ **8.** Mark studies Swedish for five years.

_____ **9.** At the moment, I am reading a fashion magazine.

_____ **10.** I like to discuss current events, so I read several newspapers every day.

GRAMMAR IN CONTEXT

Notice how the verb forms and time words in the following paragraph show time changes. Underline all of the verbs in the present.

New York City has the most people of all cities in the United States. Its population has been the largest in the United States since 1790. Currently, nearly 10 million people are living in the city. New York City is an important location for business, finance, culture, fashion, and entertainment. It has been important internationally since the United Nations was located there in 1950. Many places in the city have become popular for tourists to visit. Some of these include the Statue of Liberty, the Empire State Building, the New York Stock Exchange, Harlem, and Greenwich Village. Since September 11, 2001, many tourists have visited the site of the terrorist attacks on the World Trade Center. Therefore, the city is developing parts of this area as a memorial to the victims of the tragedy.

Forming the Simple Present—Regular Verbs

To form the simple present in third-person singular, you can usually just add only an –s.

SUBJECT	VERB	
I/You/We/They	**run**	daily.
He/She/It	**runs**	

Remember the following exceptions.

1. If the verb ends in –*ch*, –*sh*, –*ss*, –*x*, or –*zz*, add –*es*.

> wat**ch** — wat**ches**
> wa**sh** — wa**shes**
> ki**ss** — ki**sses**
> mi**x** — mi**xes**
> bu**zz** — bu**zzes**

2. If the verb ends in a consonant + –*y*, drop the –*y* and add –*ies*.

> carr**y** — carr**ies**
> tr**y** — tr**ies**

3. If the verb ends in a vowel + –*y*, just add –*s*.

> p**ay** — p**ays**
> enj**oy** — enj**oys**

Forming the Simple Present—Irregular Verbs

SUBJECT	BE	
I	**am**	
He/She/It	**is**	hungry.
We/You/They	**are**	

SUBJECT	HAVE	
I/You/We/They	**have**	
He/She/It	**has**	a problem.

SUBJECT	DO	
I/You/We/They	**do**	
He/She/It	**does**	the work quickly.

Forming Simple Present Questions and Negatives

In questions and negatives, use the auxiliary verb *do* or *does* + the base form of the main verb except when the verb is *be*. Notice that the auxiliary *do* is also used when the main verb is *do*.

QUESTION	NEGATIVE
Do you **like** old movies?	I usually **don't like** old movies.
Does Avery **go** to school every day?	No, she **does not** go to school every day.
Do you usually **do** your homework after class?	No, I **don't do** my homework until after dinner.
Is he a student?	He **isn't** a student now.

Remember:
When you use *does*, do not add –s to the verb.
Correct: *Does Avery go to school every day?*
Incorrect: *Does Avery goes to school every day?*

Self Check 1
Circle the correct form of the simple present.

1. My sister (don't / doesn't) like to read.

2. Our manager (has / have) a new computer.

3. Does Julia (speak / speaks) Spanish and Italian?

4. Mr. and Mrs. Kim (study / studies) English at night school.

5. The bank (cashs / cashes) many paychecks on Friday afternoons.

6. (He lives alone / Does he live alone) or with a roommate?

Using the Simple Present

1. Use the simple present to write about habits and routines. These are actions and situations that happen regularly.

> *I **meet** my study group weekly.*

> *Andrea **travels** a lot.*
>
> *He **washes** his laundry every weekend.*

2. Use the simple present to write about facts. These are actions and situations that are always true.

> *New Guinea **is** an island.* (fact)
>
> *The earth **revolves** around the sun.* (scientific fact)
>
> *The road **curves** very sharply.* (always true)

3. Use the simple present with non-action verbs (also called stative verbs). Non-action verbs express thoughts, feelings, senses, possession, and appearance. Avoid using these verbs in the progressive form.

Thoughts: (dis)agree, believe, know, mean, recall, remember, think (= believe), understand

> *She **believes** everything that her mother says.*

Feelings: appreciate, hate, (dis)like, love, need, prefer, want

> *I **like** chocolate ice cream more than vanilla ice cream.*

Senses: feel, hear, see, smell, taste

> *We **hear** loud music from the apartment next door.*

Possession: be, belong, have, own

> *Jae **has** three dogs at home.*

Appearance: appear, be, look, seem

> *You **look** a little tired today.*

4. Use adverbs of frequency to show the simple present when it is used to describe habits or routines.

ADVERBS OF FREQUENCY FOR HABITS AND ROUTINES		
always	never	rarely
annually	normally	regularly
daily	occasionally	seldom
every week	often	sometimes
monthly	on Fridays	usually

Adverbs of frequency come after the verb *be*. They usually come before other verbs.

> *George* **is usually** *on time for the bus.*

> *We* **rarely take** *the bus to school.*

NOTE: The simple present also has a future time use. Use it to write about scheduled events. (See Chapter 4.)

WRITING TIP

Edit carefully with the verb *remember.* Frequently, the act of remembering is in the present and the event that you remember is in the past.

Correct: *I remember the day we moved to our new home.*

Incorrect: *I remembered the day we moved to our new home.*

Self Check 2

Circle the correct form of the present.

1. Water (freezes / is freezing) at 32° Fahrenheit.

2. Steve (is belonging / belongs) to the club for economics students.

3. We (have gone / go) there all the time.

4. He usually (works / work) from a home office.

5. Fredric (is hearing / hears) his neighbor's dog daily.

Forming the Present Progressive

1. Use the simple present form of the auxiliary verb *be* (*am, is, are*) + the present participle (*–ing* form) of the main verb.

SUBJECT	VERB
I	**am leaving.**
He/She/It	**is leaving.**
You/We/They	**are leaving.**

QUESTION FORM	NEGATIVE FORM
Is he leaving?	He **isn't leaving.**
Are you leaving?	We **aren't leaving.**

2. The present progressive uses the auxiliary verb *be* + *–ing.* Do not forget the verb *be.*

> Correct: *Juan is working at the library.*

> Incorrect: *Juan working at the library.*

> Correct: *Yosuke and Lena are living close to campus.*

> Incorrect: *Yosuke and Lena living close to campus.*

WRITING TIP

Use Appendix 3 or your dictionary to check the spelling of present participles.

Self Check 3

Circle the correct form of the present progressive.

1. Paul (is drive / **is driving**) to San Francisco today.

2. Mr. Lim (**is eating** / are eating) breakfast.

3. (**Are** / Is) Ana and her sister working in a childcare center?

4. Karen (**is achieving** / is achieve) an A in the class.

5. The math homework (giving / **is giving**) me a headache.

Using the Present Progressive

1. Use the present progressive to write about actions or situations that are happening right now.

> *John **is doing** his homework now.*

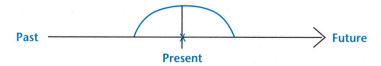

> *It's **raining**.*
>
> *They **are reviewing** the lab report at the moment.*

2. Use the present progressive to write about actions or situations that happen over an extended time in the present. The action or situation does not have to be happening right now.

> *She **is working** in a restaurant this summer.*
>
> *I'm **studying** Greek this year.*
>
> *My grandmother **is paying** my college tuition.*

3. In both of the above uses, the present progressive expresses something that is temporary. These are actions or situations with a beginning and an end. Remember to use the simple present for permanent actions or situations.

> *He **is speaking** Spanish. (This is what he is doing right now.)*
>
> *He **speaks** Spanish. (This is a permanent ability of his.)*

4. Use time words to show the present progressive. This is especially important when you change tenses.

TIME WORDS FOR THE PRESENT PROGRESSIVE				
at this moment	currently	nowadays	right now	this year/week/semester/fall
at this time	now	presently	these days	today

> *It **is beginning** to snow **now**.*
>
> *They **are currently taking** an exam.*
>
> *Yuki **is taking** photography **this year**.*

NOTE: The present progressive also has a future time use. Use it to write about future plans. (See Chapter 4.)

Self Check 4

Circle the correct form of the verb.

1. She (is knowing / knows) the correct answer to the question.

2. At this moment, Mia (listens / is listening) to her new MP3 player.

3. Americans (celebrate / are celebrating) Thanksgiving in November.

4. I (take / am taking) two history courses this semester.

5. Claudia (majors / is majoring) in chemistry.

Forming the Present Perfect

1. Use the simple present form of the auxiliary verb *have* (*have, has*) + the past participle (*–ed* form) of the main verb.

SUBJECT	VERB	
I/You/We/They	**have arrived**	on time.
He/She/It	**has arrived**	on time.

QUESTION	NEGATIVE
Have they arrived? Has she arrived?	They **haven't arrived** yet. She **hasn't** arrived.

2. Many past participles are irregular. Some of these end in *–en* (e.g., *taken, given, eaten, driven, written*). Others end in *–t* (e.g., *built, meant*). Common irregular past participles include *been, done, drunk, gone, read,* and *slept.*

> We **have gone** there many times.

> I**'ve read** that book three times.

Circle the correct form of the present perfect.

1. A jazz band (has play / has played) at Preservation Hall since the 1960s.

2. How many times (have / has) the children seen the movie *Cinderella* ?

3. Bettina and Wendy (has read / have read) all of Mark Twain's work.

4. We (have been / been) in class for two hours.

5. The professor and I (haven't discussed / hasn't discussed) my grades yet.

Using the Present Perfect

1. Use the present perfect to write about actions or situations that began in the past and continue to the present (and possibly to the future).

> I **have worked** *at the library for two years.*

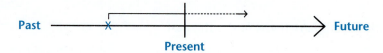

> He **has studied** *hard all week.*
>
> We **have not seen** *Todd in a long time.*

2. Use the present perfect to write about actions or situations that happened at an unspecified time in the past. (If the time is specified, use the simple past. See Chapter 2.)

> She **has** *already* **seen** *that movie.*

> They **have solved** *the problem.*
>
> I **have** *already* **eaten** *dinner.*

3. Use the present perfect to write about actions or situations that happened more than once at unspecified times in the past.

> Maria **has traveled** *to Cuba* **four times**.

> I **have been** *sick* **several times** *this winter.*
>
> It **has rained a lot** *this year.*

4. Use *for* and *since* with the present perfect to write about actions or situations that have happened over an extended period of time. *Since* tells when the time began; *for* tells the length of time it has lasted.

since + point in time:

Claire **has lived** *in Chicago* **since 2005**.

for + length of time:

The liberal party **has been** *in power* **for 10 years**.

5. In addition to *for* and *since*, use other time words to introduce the present perfect. This is especially important when you change tenses.

TIME WORDS FOR THE PRESENT PERFECT		
already	recently	until now
just	several times	yet
many	so far	

A: Have *you* **seen** *the movie* **yet**?

B: *No, I* **haven't seen** *it* **yet**. / *Yes, I've* **already seen** *it*.

He **has recently graduated** *from college*.

So far *we* **have been** *very busy*.

NOTE: *Yet* is used in questions and negative statements.

Self Check 6

Circle the word(s) that complete each sentence correctly.

1. Robert and Alvin (did not sleep / have not slept) since the day before yesterday.

2. In recent years, I (have driven / drive) the coastal highway many times.

3. He (is / has been) president for almost eight years, but soon we will have a new leader.

4. I (am / have been) very busy with work recently.

5. Mark has been gone (since / for) six months.

WRITING TIP
Be aware of the grammar errors that you make the most often and edit carefully for these problems. Use the editing log in Appendix 6 to keep track of your most common errors.

EDITING PRACTICE

1. *Put a check (✓) next to the sentences that use verb tenses correctly. Correct the sentences that have errors. Use the simple present, present progressive, or present perfect.*

_____ **1.** The communications industry becomes more competitive recently.

_____ **2.** The story is about family relationships.

_____ **3.** He has already went to school.

_____ **4.** I have not live long enough to experience everything.

_____ **5.** My family has noticed many differences between China and the United States since we arrived here in 2006.

_____ **6.** Her 100-year-old neighbor has traveled to many different countries and still remembered everything.

_____ **7.** The weather seems a little humid today.

_____ **8.** Helen is studies biology now.

_____ **9.** I am believing I did well on the midterm.

_____ **10.** We make many friends since we moved into the dorm.

_____ **11.** The earth has been round.

_____ **12.** I have not been to Canada.

2. *In the following essay, the underlined verbs are not correct. Write the correct verb form above each underlined verb. Use the simple present, present progressive, or present perfect.*

In many parts of the world, children leave home for the first time when they go away to college. A student's first year at college <u>was</u> often difficult.

From the time children are born, they <u>are depending</u> on their parents for food, clean clothing, and emotional support. After a few weeks at college, first-year students learn they have to take care of these things by themselves. They learn some difficult lessons as they become independent. However, independence also <u>is bringing</u> good things such as freedom, no curfew, and fewer household chores.

As a college freshman, I <u>go through</u> these changes right now. Since I
4

moved into the college dormitory, I <u>talk</u> to my parents a lot. Sometimes I
5

still <u>am wanting</u> their advice and support. Currently, I <u>try</u> to focus on my
6   7

schoolwork, but it is hard to study when many other students in my dorm are

not studying. They often <u>are playing</u> loud music while I am trying to study.
8

In the past, my mother always helped me focus on my homework. Without

her help, I <u>do</u> poorly on three tests so far. Even with these problems, I
9

<u>am knowing</u> that my college experiences will make me a strong person.
10

3. *Read the following paragraph. Complete the paragraph with the correct form of each verb. Use the simple present, present progressive, or present perfect.*

One of the most important influences in life _____ the
                                                                        1. be

family. People who have strong families may have an easier time succeeding,

while people with weak families may have to work harder for success.

Everyone _____ the family in a different way, and this is
                    2. describe

especially true in modern society. Traditional families include grandparents,

aunts, uncles, and cousins. However, over the past several decades this

description _____. Since the 1960s, the individual
                    3. change

_____ more important, and the traditional family
        4. become

_____ many changes. For example, nowadays, many
        5. have

children _____ in a home with one parent. In addition,
                    6. live

modern families _____ problems such as divorce, poverty,
                            7. face

and teenage pregnancy. Even though families _____ in
                                                            8. change

recent years, their basic duties _____ the same. The most
                                                9. stay

important duties of a family are the care of the youngest and oldest family

members, and these _____ the same over the past decades.
                    10. remain

4. *The following essay has ten errors in the use of the present. Find and correct the errors.*

In recent years, academic success becomes the most important goal in many countries. As a result, competition among students and among their parents has increased. This competition recently causes problems for many young people. Until now, this leads to several societal problems, including suicide. Currently, suicide increases among students in some countries where academic pressure is high. Many students are failing classes because of stress and not because of little knowledge or effort. However, this academic competition is making very educated and productive societies in many parts of the world.

Since I arrived in the United States, I am noticing that academic success is not important to all Americans. Although American society is successful, the importance of academic success is not being as strong as it is in some other countries. This may be because the United States has many different cultures, and each culture defines success in a different way. In fact, for many years, American universities are considering a student's school and community involvement in addition to grades. As a result, students are well rounded but may be academically below students in other countries. American educators now try to raise their students' academic levels.

All educational systems have positive and negative parts. We are needing a combination of the good parts from systems all over the world to make one completely successful educational program.

WRITING TOPICS

Read the student paragraph about a morning routine. Circle all of the verb forms in the present. Notice that the paragraph includes a clear topic sentence, supporting sentences, and a concluding sentence. Use this paragraph as a model when you write a paragraph about one of the topics below.

I have followed the same routine in the morning since I started attending college. I usually complete these steps each day so that I arrive at school on time and do the best work that I can. First, I exercise every morning after I get up. I run about 5 miles three days a week and swim at the community pool on the other mornings. This exercise makes me feel good and also helps me wake up in the morning. After I get home, I take a shower and get ready for school. While I am getting ready, the coffee is brewing. Next, I have a cup of coffee and eat breakfast while I am reviewing my homework for the day. I have learned that reviewing the work for my upcoming classes helps me focus on my lessons and improves my grades at school. Finally, I get in my car and drive to school. This routine made me a good student. I plan to follow this same routine when I start working because it allows me to do my best work all day.

Choose one of the topics and write one paragraph. Use mostly verbs in the present. After you complete your first draft, edit your work. Keep in mind the editing practice from this chapter.

1. Most people have a routine that they follow in the morning as they prepare for the day. Briefly describe your routine.

2. Explain why you are studying English. Include how long you have spoken or studied the language and how much your English skills have improved.

Go to page 107 for more practice with present tenses.

Expressing Past Time

GRAMMAR FOCUS

The three verb tenses discussed in this chapter—the simple past, the past progressive, and the past perfect—all express past time. However, the three tenses have different uses. Notice how they are used in the sentences below according to the time word that is chosen.

SIMPLE PAST	He **went** to the movies last night.
PAST PROGRESSIVE	We **were living** in Indonesia two years ago.
PAST PERFECT	I **had seen** that movie many times before.

Pretest

Check your understanding of the tenses that express past time. Put a check next to the sentences that are correct.

_____ **1.** We had finished all of the Thanksgiving leftovers yesterday.

_____ **2.** Carol returned her car to the repair shop because they were not fixing the brakes.

_____ **3.** When I saw the football team, they were lifting weights.

_____ **4.** The boys bought a CD by a band they didn't hear before.

_____ **5.** The two thieves seemed sorry for their actions.

_____ **6.** Last summer while I had studied in Costa Rica, I saw a rainforest for the first time.

_____ **7.** In class, the students participated in discussions.

_____ **8.** Raymond was never flying in a small airplane before last month.

_____ **9.** My aunt and I saw the Tower of London on our vacation two years ago.

_____ **10.** The day before yesterday, Tom had gone to bed earlier than usual.

GRAMMAR IN CONTEXT

Read the paragraph. Circle the verbs in the past.

After the United States had bought much of the western U.S. from the French in 1803, there was a lot of interest in this area of land. The U.S. president, Thomas Jefferson, supported an expedition to explore this region. He chose Meriwether Lewis and William Clark to lead the first expedition across the United States. These men crossed the country by both boat and foot from the east coast to the Pacific. While Lewis, Clark, and their men were exploring the United States from 1803-1806, they gathered important information about the country's plants, animals, people, and land. At the time, the expedition was a huge success, and people still study the information that Lewis and Clark learned over 200 years ago.

Forming the Simple Past

1. For most verbs, add *–ed* or *–d* to the base form for the simple past. This is true for all subjects (*I, you, he, she, it, we, they*, etc.).

clean — *clean**ed***

dance — *danc**ed***

look — *look**ed***

live — *live**d***

wash — *wash**ed***

believe — *believe**d***

2. Many common verbs are irregular in the simple past.

SUBJECT	BE	
I/He/She/It	**was**	in Hong Kong last year.
You/We/They	**were**	in Hong Kong last year.

Some other irregular verbs are:

do — **did**

have — **had**

come — **came**

go — **went**

buy — **bought**

eat — **ate**

run — **ran**

take — **took**

NOTE: All irregular verbs expect for *be* have the same simple past form for all subjects.

3. In questions and negatives, use the auxiliary verb *did* + the base form of the main verb except when the verb is *be*.

> **Did** you **go** to the party last night?
>
> When **did** you **see** Martha?
>
> I **did not take** a vacation last year.

But with the verb *be*:

> **Were** you happy with the results?

WRITING TIP

Use Appendix 2 or your dictionary to make sure that you are using the correct form of a verb that is irregular in the simple past.

Self Check 1

Circle the correct simple past form of the verb.

1. Richard and I (did not completed / did not complete) our homework.

2. When (did Katherine and Lee finish / Katherine and Lee finished) the test?

3. Darla (seen / saw) a movie with her friend last night.

4. Who (Dr. Lawler chose / did Dr. Lawler choose) for the job?

5. We (was / were) not lucky in Las Vegas last weekend.

Using the Simple Past

1. Use the simple past to write about completed actions and situations. These actions and situations ended in the past and have no connection to the present. They can be habits or refer to a point in time or a period in time.

> I wrote a ten-page paper last semester.

Past ⟶ ✗ —————————|—————————⟶ **Future**

Present

> They **went** to the prom last year. (point in time)
>
> We **lived** in Mexico for three years. (period of time)
>
> As a child, I **watched** a lot of TV. (habitual)

2. Use time words to show the simple past. This is especially important when you change tenses. Use a comma when one of these words or phrases begins a sentence.

TIME WORDS FOR THE SIMPLE PAST		
a few minutes ago	in the past	the day before yesterday
in 1980	last week	yesterday

> A deliveryman **came** to the office **yesterday**.
>
> **Yesterday**, we **decided** to sell our house.
>
> My friend **arrived** at the airport **two hours ago**.
>
> **In 1980**, we **travelled** to Ecuador.

3. *Used to* and *would* can be used for actions and situations that were habits in the past. Use *used to* to show a contrast with the present. *Used to* is more common than *would*. Both *used to* and *would* are followed by the base form of the main verb.

> When I was a child, I **used to eat** (or) **would eat** a lot of candy.
>
> Melody doesn't study much now, but she **used to study** a lot.

Self Check 2

Circle the correct form of the verb.

1. In high school, I used to (watching / watch) a lot of TV.

2. A few years ago, Yutaka (saw / seen) his first American football game.

3. François (spoke / speaks) only French when he lived in France.

4. They (went out / would go out) to dinner last night.

5. Janna texts her friends now, but she (used to / would) call them more often.

Forming the Past Progressive

Use the simple past form of the auxiliary verb *be* (*am, is, are*) + the present participle (*–ing* form) of the main verb.

SUBJECT	VERB	
I/He/She/It	**was sitting**	in the garden.
You/We/They	**were sitting**	in the garden.

> ### WRITING TIP
> Use Appendix 3 or your dictionary to check the spelling of present participles.

Self Check 3

Circle the correct form of the past progressive.

1. Ronald was (take / taking) a pronunciation class, but he dropped it last week.

2. I was (study / studying) in the library this morning.

3. Parisa and Tarik (was / were) practicing their oral presentation last night.

4. Last spring, we (was travel / were traveling) around Europe and Asia.

5. She (does not / was not) walking her dog during the rainstorm yesterday.

Using the Past Progressive

1. Use the past progressive to write about actions and situations that were in progress at a specific time in the past.

At ten o'clock last night, I **was studying** *for an exam.*

In 1995, she **was living** *in Washington, D.C.*

At the time the Berlin Wall fell, Aaron **was traveling** *in Germany.*

2. Use the past progressive to write about actions or situations that were interrupted by another past action. Express the interrupting action in the simple past. Use *while* with the past progressive and *when* with the simple past.

While *I* **was eating** *dinner, the coach* **called**.

or

I was **eating dinner when** *the coach* **called**.

3. Use the past progressive to emphasize that an action or situation is ongoing—in progress over a period of time—or temporary. In contrast, the simple past emphasizes that an action or situation is completed.

Last December, Tiffany **was failing** *the course.* (Tiffany was failing at that point in time; perhaps she did not fail the course.)

Last December, Tiffany **failed** *the course.* (Tiffany definitely failed the course.)

4. Use the simple past, not the past progressive, with non-action verbs. (See page 15.)

During the test, I **knew** *all of the answers.*

5. In addition to *when* and *while*, use a variety of time words to show the past progressive. This is especially important when you change tenses.

TIME WORDS FOR THE PAST PROGRESSIVE		
as	at that time	during
at that moment	at the time	in the 1950s/1990s

As *we* **were walking** *out the door, the telephone* **rang**.

The Beatles and the Rolling Stones **were recording** *albums* **in the 1960s**.

WRITING TIP

A learner's dictionary will tell you if a verb is normally used in the progressive form.

Self Check 4

Circle the correct form of the verb.

1. Hugh (had / was having) many friends by the end of the semester.

2. I saw my favorite professor while he (ate / was eating) lunch.

3. At eleven o'clock this morning, she (still slept / was still sleeping).

4. On the second day of the semester, Igor (was joining / joined) the class.

5. We were singing a song when the fireworks (were beginning / began).

Forming the Past Perfect

1. Use the simple past form of the auxiliary verb *have* (*had*) + the past participle
   (*–ed* form) of the main verb.

SUBJECT	VERB	
I/You/He/She/It/We/They	**had studied**	before the final exam.

2. Many past participles are irregular. Some of these end in *–en* (*taken, given, eaten, driven, written,* etc.). Others end in *–t* (*built, meant,* etc.). Common irregular past participles include *been, done, drunk, gone, read,* and *slept*.

   We **had gone** *to the island before the storm destroyed its beauty.*

> **WRITING TIP**
>
> Use Appendix 2 or your dictionary to make sure you have the correct form of the past participle.

Self Check 5

Circle the correct form of the past perfect.

1. The child had (run / ran) into the street many times before his mother punished him.

2. By the time the movie started, we (have / had) seen six movie previews.

3. The class had (start / started) by 8:00 A.M.

4. The university had (gave / given) out all of its scholarships before the deadline.

5. Mrs. Costello (had not / did not had) taught English before she moved to Korea.

Using the Past Perfect

1. Use the past perfect to write about past action or situation that happened before another past action. Use the simple past for the more recent action.

   *The rain **had stopped** by the time we **left**.*

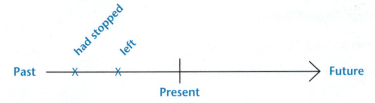

   *The students **had read** [first] the book before they **saw** [second] the movie.*

   *Before they **saw** [second] the movie, they **had read** [first] the book.*

2. Use the past perfect to write about actions and situations that happened before a specific time in the past.

   *Susan **had never seen** so many beautiful flowers **before that day**.*

   When the class ended**, he **had already left.

3. The simple past can often replace the past perfect with no change in meaning.

   *She went to dinner after she **had finished** her work.*

   *She went to dinner after **she finished** her work.*

NOTE: When only one past event is mentioned in a sentence, use the simple past, not the past perfect.

   *We **used** a dictionary during the test.*

                              not

   We had used a dictionary during the test.

4. Use time words to show the past perfect. This is especially important when you change tenses.

TIME WORDS FOR THE PAST PERFECT			
after	at that time	by then	until
already when	before	by the time	

   *Mrs. Long **had gone** to the theater **when** we **called** her.*

   *Jenny's parents **had given** her a car **by the time** she **was** eighteen. However, they **had not given** her brother a car **until** he **was** twenty-one.*

WRITING TIP
Underline all time words in your writing, and make sure the verb tenses agree with the time words.

Circle the letter of the sentence that uses past verb forms correctly.

1. **a.** Joan's friend had left the theater before the movie had ended.

   b. Joan's friend had left the theater before the movie ended.

2. **a.** Grace had realized that she had left the house unlocked.

   b. Grace realized that she had left the house unlocked.

3. **a.** By the time Honda offered John a job, he had accepted another job.

   b. By the time Honda offered John a job, he accepted another job.

4. **a.** We had attended the last class yesterday.

   b. We attended the last class yesterday.

5. **a.** The little boy had not seen a real lion before that day.

   b. The little boy did not see a real lion before that day.

WRITING TIP

Wait several hours or days between writing and editing your work. This extra time will help you spot your errors more easily.

EDITING PRACTICE

1. *Put a check (✓) next to the sentences that use past verb forms correctly. Correct the sentences that have errors. Use the simple past, past progressive, or past perfect.*

_____ **1.** I understood my country's problems and why we have to move away

two years ago.

_____ **2.** She has gone to several concerts last month.

_____ **3.** When Brandon was a child, he would spend every summer with his

grandparents.

_____ **4.** When we first moved here, we had felt lonely.

_____ **5.** Lauren was taking the exam when she heard her cell phone ring.

_____ **6.** Jun and Chris had seen the new play last night.

_____ **7.** My mother was preparing for a dinner party at 11:30 last night.

_____ **8.** They had arrived in San Diego by the time I was getting there.

_____ **9.** My family was having three dogs.

_____ **10.** While they had lived in the mountains, they saw bears in their

backyard.

_____ **11.** He was never taking a speech class before the class he took last semester.

_____ **12.** Marti does not dance a lot now, but she used to be a professional dancer.

2. _In the following paragraph, the underlined verbs are not correct. Write the correct verb form above each underlined verb. Use the simple past, past progressive, or past perfect._

My aunt is the best example of a hard worker. When she first arrived in

the United States, she <u>does not know</u> any English. She also knew very little
₁

about business in this country. She learned English while she <u>had taken</u>
₂

business classes. After school she <u>had studied</u>. In addition, she worked at
₃

a small company in the evening. Because of all her hard work, she

<u>was graduating</u> with a business degree. She also <u>overcome</u> other difficulties.
₄   ₅

During that time, the economy <u>did</u> poorly, and it was hard for her to find a
₆

job. Finally she <u>had found</u> a good one. She worked at that job for five years.
₇

Then she <u>was quitting</u> for a better job. She started her new position last year,
₈

and after six months, her boss promoted her to a higher position. She

<u>was being</u> very happy with the promotion. My aunt is my role model because
₉

she followed her dream when all of her effort <u>does not pay off</u> right away.
₁₀

Now she is successful and satisfied because all of her hard work has improved

her life.

3. _Read the following paragraph. Complete the paragraph with the correct past form of each verb. Use the simple past or past progressive._

At some point in life, most people can say that they are mature.

I believe that I _____ at a young age. I _____
_{**1. mature**}   _{**2. become**}

mature when my family left our country. While we _____
_{**3. fly**}

to the United States, my father told me that I had to communicate for the whole family. I was only fourteen years old. Neither of my parents spoke English, and five years ago, I _____ very little English,

4. know

but it was more than the others in my family. For weeks, while my father

_____ for a place for us to live, I had to translate for him.

5. look

While my younger sisters _____ to their new school,

6. adjust

I _____ there to help them. Over the next few months,

7. be

while my parents, grandparents, and siblings _____ about

8. learn

our new home, I _____ bigger responsibilities. Although I

9. have

_____ a lot, I wish that I had had a little longer to be a

10. learn

child.

4. *The following paragraph has ten errors in the use of the past. Find and correct the errors.*

Today I still remembered the start of my longest friendship. It began in fourth grade. There was a girl in my class named Sandi. She was being the student who did not always raise her hand and who talked loudly in class. One day Sandi asked me to help her with her homework. I did not wanted to help her, but I didn't know how to say *no*. I choosed not to answer her question. I was working quietly when she told the teacher that I was her new homework partner. I disliked Sandi, and I was not wanting to ignore her question any longer. I had ignored her for as long as I could. I walked up to Sandi and told her I did not want to help her with her homework. No one had ever said *no* to her before, so she was looking very surprised. The teacher had heard our conversation, and she came over to talk to me. She asked for my help with Sandi, so I had agreed to be her partner. After I had work with Sandi for a few days, I was learning that she was very nice, and I had judged her too quickly. It's amazing that we are still friends today when you think about how our friendship had started.

WRITING TOPICS

Read the student paragraph about leaving for college. Circle all of the verb forms in the past. Notice that this paragraph includes a clear topic sentence, supporting sentences, and a concluding sentence. Use this paragraph as a model when you write a paragraph about one of the topics below.

After I graduated from high school, I decided to go to a university in another state. I was excited about this decision, but I had not anticipated the mixed emotions I felt the day that I left home. As I was packing my possessions for school, I already missed my family. I knew that I was going to see my family in a few months, but I felt very lonely when I was driving away from home the first time. I felt sad for the entire five-hour drive to my new school. When I got there, my emotions changed from sadness to excitement. I met my roommate and many of the other students who were moving into my dormitory. We all came from different parts of the country and had very different backgrounds. I was interested in learning about everyone, and I forgot about my loneliness. Throughout my first months away from home, I missed my family and felt homesick at times, but it was never as bad as the first day. Although this experience was difficult, it showed me that the excitement of new experiences can help ease sadness.

Choose one of the topics and write one paragraph. Use mostly verbs in the past. After you complete your first draft, edit your work. Keep in mind the editing practice from this chapter.

1. Describe the first day you lived away from your home or your family. What was the day like, and how did you feel? Explain your reasons for leaving your home or your family.

2. Throughout our lives, we are influenced by people around us. Describe a time in your life when you were influenced by another person or group of people. The influence can be either positive or negative. What was happening in your life at that time?

Go to page 109 for more practice with past tenses.

Subject-Verb Agreement

GRAMMAR FOCUS

A verb must agree with its subject. It must agree in person (first person = *I, we;* second person = *you;* third person = *he, she, it, they*) and in number (singular or plural). Notice how the subjects and verbs agree in both person and number in the following sentences.

SINGULAR SUBJECTS AND VERBS	PLURAL SUBJECTS AND VERBS
I am studying.	**We are** studying.
You are studying.	**You are** studying.
He is studying.	**They are** studying.
His brother lives in Oregon.	**The children live** in Oregon.
It tastes good.	**These strawberries taste** good.
She works hard.	**John and his sister work** hard.

Pretest

Check your understanding of subject-verb agreement. Put a check (✓) next to the sentences that are correct.

_____ **1.** India and China have fast-growing populations.

_____ **2.** There are a lot of good movies that I want to see.

_____ **3.** Carrie and Kay is planning the school elections.

_____ **4.** The elections was very successful last year.

_____ **5.** Do Benjamin live in a house or an apartment?

_____ **6.** Travelling to new cities are so much fun.

_____ **7.** My parents have helped me succeed in life.

_____ **8.** Our friend plays classical guitar beautifully.

_____ **9.** The drama department offers fun classes.

_____ **10.** One of her favorite flowers come from South America.

GRAMMAR IN CONTEXT

Read the paragraph. Circle the subjects and underline the verbs. Notice how the verbs agree with their subjects.

Education in the United States is available to adults in several different places. Many students choose four-year universities or colleges after high school. Some students don't have good grades or cannot afford to pay for four-year colleges. These students can finish their first two years of college at a community college and then transfer to a four-year university or college. Some adults go to adult school because they need to finish their high school degree or improve their English before they go to a community college or four-year university. Adult school also offers certificates in areas like computers, business, and early childhood development. One of the benefits of education in the United States is the many choices that adults have.

Subject-Verb Agreement: Form

SIMPLE PRESENT
Be **I am** ready. **He/She/It is** ready. **We/You/They are** ready.
Regular Verbs **I/You/We/They work.** **He/She/It works.**

PRESENT PROGRESSIVE
I am working. **You/We/They are** working. **He/She/It is** working.

PRESENT PERFECT
I/You/We/They have eaten. **He/She/It has** eaten.

SIMPLE PAST
Be **I/He/She/It was** late. **You/We/They were** late.
Regular Verbs **I/You/He/She/It/We/They worked.** Note: There are many irregular verbs in the simple past. See page 15.

PAST PROGRESSIVE
I/He/She/It was eating. **You/We/They were** eating.

Circle the correct form of the verb.

1. The birds (were / was) flying south for the winter.

2. We (be / are) happy with our test scores.

3. Alexander (are / is) taking too many units this semester.

4. Babies (cries / cry) a lot on airplanes.

5. Mobile phones (have / has) been popular since the 1990s.

Rules for Subject-Verb Agreement

1. A verb must agree with its subject.

   *Those **dogs are** really cute.*

2. The subject is not always the noun nearest the verb. Subjects and verbs may be separated by a phrase or clause.

   *The **dogs** in the pet store **are** really cute.*

   ***Adanna and Adwin**, who came from Africa last year, **live** next door.*

3. When the subject is two or more nouns joined by *and*, use a plural verb.

   ***Tacos and pizza have** always been my favorite foods.*

   ***Australia, Mexico, and France produce** delicious cheese.*

4. If the subject of a sentence is *one of the* + plural noun, the main subject is *one* and the verb is singular.

   ***One** of the students **has** the flu.*

5. If the subject of a sentence is *none of the* + plural noun or *neither/either of the* + plural noun, the main subject is singular and the verb is singular.

   ***None** of the teams **is** playing well.*

   ***Neither** of the dates **is** convenient for us.*

   ***Either** of the books **contains** the information that you need.*

6. In sentences with *there* + *be*, the subject is the noun following *be*. If the noun is singular, use the singular form (*is/was*) of *be*. If the noun is plural, use the plural form (*are/were*) of *be*.

   *There **is** a good **show** on TV tonight.*

   *There **has been** a lot of **crime** in our neighborhood recently.*

   *There **are ants** all over the kitchen.*

7. Gerunds (verb + *–ing*) and infinitives (*to* + verb) as subjects use the third-person singular form of the verb.

   ***Skiing is** Lydia's favorite sport.*

   *For some people, **shopping has become** an obsession.*

   ***Discussing** politics **causes** arguments in many families.*

   ***To live** in a foreign country **is** my dream.*

   ***To get** front-row tickets **costs** a lot of money.*

Underline the subjects and verbs in each sentence you write. Make sure they agree.

Self Check 2

Circle the verb that agrees with the subject.

1. Recycling garbage and paper (help / helps) the environment.

2. There (are / is) snow in Toronto and Quebec.

3. The books that we read in English class (are / is) classics.

4. Yoga, tai chi, and meditation (helps / help) people's concentration.

5. One of the airplanes (are / is) late.

EDITING PRACTICE

1. *Put a check (✓) next to the sentences that use subject-verb agreement correctly. Correct the sentences that have errors.*

_____ 1. Some students has test anxiety before important exams.

_____ 2. Having high-tech skills is useful in the workplace today.

_____ 3. The sofa and chair costs too much.

_____ 4. There is many times when I don't feel confident at school.

_____ 5. My family and I was happy when we left our very poor country.

_____ 6. Some people take advantage of the welfare system.

_____ 7. To study for final exams is better with a study group.

_____ 8. New laws requires businesses to pay more taxes.

_____ 9. None of the computers have enough memory.

_____ 10. What industries help the economy the most?

_____ 11. Neither of the planes leave before noon.

_____ 12. Oil prices goes down when there is a large supply.

_____ 13. One of the best fairy tales is "Cinderella."

_____ 14. Common illnesses like the flu has killed millions of people.

_____ 15. Jogging and swimming are good ways to exercises.

2. *In the following paragraph, the underlined verbs are not correct. Write the correct verb form above each underlined verb.*

It is important to understand the writing process. First, students need to

practice good writing habits. After watching many of my friends, I <u>has</u> found
1

that there <u>is</u> common characteristics that good writers have. Most students
2

in high school and college <u>is</u> good writers when they want to be, but they
3

usually <u>puts</u> it off until the last minute. Then they don't have enough time
4

to do a good job. Some students do the second draft immediately after the

first, even though the teacher <u>ask</u> for the drafts a week apart. Good writers
5

use the first draft to explore ideas. They <u>waits</u> a few hours or days before
6

beginning the second draft. Then they <u>becomes</u> the editor and revise the
7

ideas in the paper. A good essay <u>go</u> through many revisions. One of the best
8

revision techniques <u>are</u> asking another student to read the essay. All students
9

should follow the writing process to become good writers. Good writing and

revising only <u>comes</u> after a lot of time and practice.
10

3. *Read the following paragraph. Complete the paragraph with the correct form of each verb.*

There _____ many qualities that make a good leader. It
1. be

doesn't matter if the leader _____ a country, a high school,
2. lead

or a family. The same qualities _____ always necessary.
3. be

Good leadership _____ flexibility, understanding, and
4. require

honesty. Many people _____ some of these qualities,
5. have

but only a few people have all of them and the desire to be a great leader.

Flexibility _____ one of the most important qualities.
6. be

Without the ability to change an idea or plan, a leader will not be successful.

In addition to flexibility, another important quality _____

7. be

understanding. All outstanding leaders _____ the ability to

8. have

put themselves in the place of others. Finally, honesty _____

9. have

to be a part of a great leader's personality. Leaders who win our trust are the

most successful. Having these three qualities _____ what

10. be

makes a leader great.

4. *The following paragraph has ten errors in subject–verb agreement. Find and correct the errors.*

When I first entered high school, I met my best friend, Chong.

Throughout our four years in high school, we was best friends. Now that we

are away at different universities, our friendship and affection has grown

stronger. We communicates daily through e-mail, texting, and phone calls.

These helps us stay in touch over a long distance. Chong is at the University

of Chicago, and I am at the University of Southern California, so it is difficult

for us to communicate in person. I think my best friend feel lonely in Illinois;

therefore, I always takes the time to keep in touch with him. We like to

remember the many experiences that we have had together. One of the most

memorable events were during our senior year. We had the physics final

exam, but neither of us had studied for it. There was many times we competed

against each other, but those times helped us build a strong friendship. I

know Chong cherish our relationship as much as I do. We are both majoring

in biology and planning to go to the same graduate school. Being apart now

have made our friendship stronger for the future.

WRITING TOPICS

Read the student paragraph about a beautiful place. Underline five examples of subjects and their verbs. Notice that the paragraph includes a clear topic sentence, supporting sentences, and a concluding sentence. Use this paragraph as a model when you write a paragraph about one of the topics below.

During the summertime, the areas surrounding Seattle, Washington, are the most beautiful in the world. The colors are amazing in this area. The sky is bright blue and has big white clouds. The whole area seems to be covered with the greenest trees while the mountains have bright white snow on the peaks. Besides the colors, the waterways that surround Seattle are the most beautiful in the world. The cold water is so clear in places that it is possible to see orange starfish, yellow jellyfish, and red sea anemones. There are many small islands that are covered with trees and nice beaches. The natural beauty of Seattle is fantastic, but downtown Seattle has many pretty neighborhoods, too. The old buildings in Pioneer Square were built of brick and stone in the late nineteenth century. Their style makes this old neighborhood very charming. There are also many modern skyscrapers in the downtown area. The residential neighborhoods that surround downtown have a lot of old wooden homes that were built 50 to 100 years ago. All of these different building styles make the city and its neighborhoods so beautiful. Because the Seattle area has so much natural and manmade beauty, it is one of the prettiest places in the world.

Choose one of the topics and write at least one paragraph. Use a variety of subjects, and make sure the subjects and verbs agree. After you complete your first draft, concentrate on editing your work. Keep in mind the editing practice from this chapter.

1. There are many beautiful places in the world such as the beach, the mountains, the desert, or the downtown of a large city. In your opinion, what is the most beautiful place in the world? Describe this place and its beauty.

2. People around the world celebrate many different holidays. What is your favorite holiday? In which country or countries is it celebrated? Why is this holiday important? What activities, people, food, and traditions are a part of the celebration?

Go to page 111 for more practice with subject–verb agreement.

4 Expressing Future Time

GRAMMAR FOCUS

There are four ways to express future time in English: *will* + verb, *be going to* + verb, the present progressive, and the simple present. Each of these forms can be used to write about actions and situations that will happen at some time in the future, but each is used in different situations. Notice how the following four sentences express future time but use a different form of the verb to do this.

WILL + BASE FORM	We **will get** there at about ten o'clock.
BE GOING TO + BASE FORM	I **am going to take** a class next month.
PRESENT PROGRESSIVE	I **am eating** at Ki's house tonight.
SIMPLE PRESENT	Our plane **leaves** at five o'clock.

Pretest

Check your understanding of verbs that express future time. Put a check (✓) next to the sentences that are correct.

_____ **1.** I won't register for the history class until next week.

_____ **2.** When Ti-lien will give her speech, she will use a computer.

_____ **3.** Our neighbor leaving for vacation this Saturday.

_____ **4.** Mr. Jackson gardens later this afternoon.

_____ **5.** Ji promises that next year she will submit her taxes early.

_____ **6.** According to the weather report, it is raining on Friday.

_____ **7.** Dave and Kevin are going to watch their favorite TV show at ten o'clock tonight.

_____ **8.** We buy a new house next winter.

_____ **9.** He studies the formulas before he takes the exam next week.

_____ **10.** Before we cook dinner tonight, we are going to take a walk.

GRAMMAR IN CONTEXT

Read the paragraph. Notice how the writer indicates future time through the use of verbs and time words. Underline all of the verbs that express future time.

Within the next few years, the university is going to have a new library. The old library will become a large lecture hall. The new library will be five stories tall and have a lot of study rooms, computers, and comfortable reading chairs. Many of the old books and resources will not be in the new library because it is going to have more online resources. The librarians are going to teach classes about using the online resources that the new library will have. They also plan to hire more student assistants to help with the new technology. Construction of the library starts soon and finishes in two years.

Forming Future Time Verbs

1. Use *will* + the base form of the verb for all subjects. Do not add an *–s* for third-person singular subjects. The negative form is *will not* or *won't*.

SUBJECT	VERB	
I/You/He/She/It/We/They	**will leave**	next week.
I/You/He/She/It/We/They	**will not leave/won't leave**	next week.

2. Use the simple present form of *be* (*am, is, are*) + *going to* + the base form of the verb.

SUBJECT	VERB	
I	**am going to finish**	soon.
He/She/It	**is going to finish**	soon.
You/We/They	**are going to finish**	soon.

3. Use the simple present form of *be* + the present participle (*–ing* form) of the verb. (For more on forming the present progressive, see Chapter 1.)

4. Add *–s* to the base form with third-person singular subjects. Use the base form of the verb for all other subjects. (For more on forming the simple present, see Chapter 1.)

5. In future statements with *will*, *be going to*, or the present progressive where *and* is used to connect two actions for the same subject, it is not necessary to repeat the auxiliary verb.

> *John **will win** the race and **come** home happy.*

> *I'm going to have** dinner with Elena tomorrow and **tell** her the good news.*

or

> *I'm having** dinner with Elena tomorrow and **telling** her about my new job.*

Circle the correct form of the verb.

1. My teacher (don't / won't) accept late homework.

2. A new computer will (changes / change) your life.

3. They (are going to eat / going to eat) dinner early tonight.

4. Mrs. Ko's plane (leaves / leave) at nine o'clock tomorrow morning.

5. We (dining / are dining) at the new restaurant on Friday night.

Using the Future

1. Use *will* to make predictions about the future.

> *John* **will** *win the race.*

When you are less certain about a prediction, use words such as *probably, maybe,* or *perhaps.*

> *John* **will probably** *win the race.*

> or

> **Maybe** *John* **will** *win the race.*

2. Use *will* to make promises, offers, and requests. This shows your willingness to do something.

> *I* **will be** *there.* (promise)

> *I'***ll take** *you to the doctor's office.* (offer)

> **Will** *you* **do** *me a favor?* (request)

3. Use *be going to,* like *will,* to make predictions about the future.

> *John* **is going to win** *the race.*

> *I* **am going to have** *dinner with Elena tomorrow night.*

4. Use *be* + verb to write about plans already made for the future.

> *I'***m having** *dinner with Elena tomorrow night.*

NOTE: In a sentence about the future that has a time clause (a dependent clause beginning with a time word such as *after, before, when,* or *while*), use the simple present for the event in the time clause and use *will* or *be going to* for the event in the other clause.

> **After** *Cindy* **graduates,** *she* **will have** *more time for her hobbies.*

5. The present progressive, like *be going to,* can be used to write about plans already made for the future.

> *I'***m having** *dinner with Elena tomorrow night.*

6. Use the simple present to express future actions that are on a definite schedule or timetable (e.g., movies, trains, etc.). Verbs commonly used in the simple present for the future include *arrive*, *begin*, *depart*, *finish*, *leave*, and *start*.

   Next year school **starts** *on September 3 and* **finishes** *on June 10.*

7. Use time words to show the future. This is especially important when you change time frames and use the simple present or present progressive to express the future.

TIME WORDS TO SHOW THE FUTURE					
later	next week	soon	the day after tomorrow	tomorrow	tonight

   Our flight **leaves next Saturday at 8:00 A.M.**

   They **are leaving tomorrow for a vacation.**

WRITING TIP

Always read your essay aloud. It will help you notice things that do not make sense or sound awkward.

Self Check 2

Circle the correct form of the verb to complete the sentence.

1. The publisher thinks her new novel (sells / will sell) 1 million copies.

2. Cynthia (is going to get / gets) As in all of her classes this year.

3. A: Who can loan me $10?

   B: I (will loan / am going to loan) you the money.

4. Andrew (buys / is buying) a new car next week.

5. The bus (comes / will come) at 7:05 P.M.

EDITING PRACTICE

1. *Put a check (✓) next to the sentences that use future verbs correctly. Correct the sentences that have errors. Use* will, be going to, *simple present, or present progressive. There may be more than one way to correct an error.*

_____ **1.** Next summer I'm going to enroll in a language class.

_____ **2.** After she graduates, Anna gets a part-time job.

_____ **3.** I think that this class will be very interesting.

_____ **4.** The college president is at the meeting tomorrow.

_____ **5.** Our friends going to arrive on the next flight.

_____ **6.** Tomorrow the bus leaves at 7:00 P.M.

_____ **7.** I will sleeping like a baby tonight.

_____ **8.** We are remembering to pick you up at the airport next week.

_____ **9.** They won't not work at the same job after graduation.

_____ **10.** Some of my friends are coming to visit me next spring.

_____ **11.** Melissa will rents a house in the mountains next year.

_____ **12.** When my parents will arrive, we are going to take them out for dinner.

2. *In the following essay, the underlined verbs are not correct. Write the correct form above each underlined verb. Use* will, be going to, *the simple present, or the present progressive. There may be more than one correct form.*

I think my next summer vacation will be the best vacation of my life.

My friends and I are visiting Korea for one month. It is going to be my first

vacation without my family. First we <u>arriving</u> in Seoul and <u>stay</u> with my
                                        1   **2**

cousins for three weeks. While we <u>will be</u> in Seoul, we are going to shop a lot.
                                   3

The summer weather is very hot in Korea, so most of our time <u>do not include</u>
                                                               4

outdoor activities. After we <u>will leave</u> Seoul, we are going to stay with some
                             5

friends for a week in the countryside. Hopefully, the countryside <u>is</u> cool, so we
                                                                   6

can hike and explore the outdoors.

After one month in Korea, I am returning home to work for six weeks.

I will probably have enough time to earn some money for my school expenses.

I hope to work at my aunt's hotel business where I probably <u>gain</u> a lot of
                                                            7

useful work experience. Next year, I <u>changing my major to</u> hospitality
                                      8

management. Therefore, my travel and work experience <u>will helps</u> me after I
                                                      9

<u>will graduate</u> and start looking for work in the hospitality field.
10

3. *Read the following essay. Complete the paragraph with the correct verb forms.*

Many colleges and universities are beautiful and interesting places to visit. This is why I am looking forward to showing my university to my family next weekend. They _____ here on Saturday
                                   1. flying / are going to fly

morning. Then they _____ a car to drive
                            2. rent / are renting

to campus. Once they arrive, I am going to give them a tour of my beautiful university campus.

This is how I _____ them around. They
                     3. will show / show

are going to drive through the main gate. After they pass the main gate, they

_____ a big parking lot for visitors. When
           4. see / will see

they _____ the parking lot, they will
         5. will exit / exit

see the statue of the university's first president. Here they will notice the admissions building. This beautiful building was built in the 1800s. I predict

this _____ their favorite place on the
         6. is / will be

campus. Next, my family will walk across the science plaza where they'll see

the chemistry, biology, and physics buildings. Before we go to the library,

we are going to pass the new arboretum. Even though the university

_____ the arboretum for another few
    7. doesn't finish / won't finish

months, my father _____ to spend some
              8. is wanting / will want

time there. The botany department has wonderful greenhouses that we

_____ after we leave the library. My younger
    9. tour / are going to tour

brother and sister will want to stop at the student store and buy T-shirts.

I hope that this tour _____ my family
         10. is helping / will help

become familiar with my new life away from home.

4. *The following essay has ten errors in the use of the future. Find and correct the errors. There may be more than one way to correct some errors.*

My friends and I are planning a celebration after our very last final exam of our senior year. Immediately after we finish the last exam, we will walks to the Marketplace to celebrate. The owner of the computer arcade there promises that his arcade will be a good place to start our celebration. We spend an hour or two at the arcade before we go to Koko and Elena's. They having a party at their apartment. When we get there, we swim and eat delicious food from all over the world. Each person is going to bring one dish from his or her country. Because of this, the food is tasting interesting and delicious. We all know this is a wonderful party to celebrate our accomplishments together.

After I will say good-bye to all of my friends, I'll go home to pack my bags. I will leave the following day for a new job. Even though I don't know my exact duties now, I am going work at my uncle's company. I plan to use my English skills a lot. My uncle wants me to work with his English-speaking customers because he does not speak English well. My future home and job is going to be on another continent. This will be the third continent I have lived on. I know that I love it as much as the first two.

WRITING TOPICS

Read the student's paragraph about college life in the future. Circle all of the verb forms that express future time. Notice that the paragraph includes a clear topic sentence, supporting sentences, and a concluding sentence. Use this paragraph as a model when you write about one of the topics below.

In fifty years, college life will probably be very different. Today college students do most of their work on the college campus, but in the future there may not be any college campuses. Some people predict that students are going to take all of their classes on the computer. They will listen to lectures, ask questions, and take notes at home. Their computers will replace traditional classrooms and lecture classes. Another change will be fewer professors. They may no longer be necessary. Students are going to be able to find all the information online. Students will need professors only to answer questions and grade some papers. Finally, college tuition will be very inexpensive. Without college campuses, there will be fewer costs for the colleges. Students will not have to pay for administrative costs and professors' salaries. All of these changes will probably make college life in the future very different from how it is now.

Choose one of the topics and write at least one paragraph. Try to use all the verb forms that express future time. After you finish writing, concentrate on editing your work. Keep in mind the editing practice from this chapter.

1. In fifty years, our world will probably be very different. What do you predict the world will be like then? Describe things that will definitely happen and things that may happen. You could write about topics such as the environment, technology, business, government, or family life.

2. Select a building, a park, a city, or any other place that you are very familiar with. Pretend that you are taking a group of friends there for the first time. Think about what your friends will do while they are there and how you hope they are going to feel about this place when they leave.

Go to page 113 for more practice expressing future time.

Time Shifts and Tenses

GRAMMAR FOCUS

Writers often shift between the past, present, and future. For your readers to understand these time shifts, it is important to choose tenses carefully. Using time words to express these time shifts will also help make your writing clear. Notice how the following sentences shift between the past, present, and future and use time words to signal the changes in tense.

> Last year my sister's children came to my house every weekend, but this year I have only seen them three times so far. I know when they go to school next year, I will see them even less often.

Pretest

Check your understanding of time shifts and tense. Put a (✓) next to the sentences that are correct.

_____ **1.** Before he buys a computer, he will look for the best price.

_____ **2.** Every year the conference began May 1, so I will arrive April 30.

_____ **3.** Yulia decide to take piano lessons because she thinks piano music is so beautiful.

_____ **4.** I have seen *The Sound of Music* in the fifth grade and haven't seen it since then.

_____ **5.** Helen is at the gym now, but she is home soon.

_____ **6.** We don't see the car that you bought last month yet.

_____ **7.** Sonja looked embarrassed after she had fallen on the library stairs.

_____ **8.** Mollie was taking a film studies class this semester, so she went to the movies last night for homework.

_____ **9.** Economists believe unemployment will increase next year.

_____ **10.** Jack is finishing cleaning his room, but his mother thought it wasn't clean enough.

GRAMMAR IN CONTEXT

Read the paragraph. Notice how the writer moves between the present, past, and future. The underlined time words help to show these changes. As you read the paragraph, notice the time words and circle the verbs.

Next month the gray whales are going to begin their yearly trip from the Bering Sea down to Mexico's Baja Peninsula. They will arrive in Mexico about three to four months later. Every year, this migration begins in October and ends by February or March. The whales travel about eighty miles each day; the total trip is approximately 12,500 miles. The gray whales go to Baja to mate and to have their babies. Today the gray whales are protected, but in the past, whalers hunted them for oil and whalebone. By the 1930s almost all the gray whales were extinct. Since 1949, the International Whaling Commission has protected gray whales, so the numbers of these whales have increased significantly. Because of strong laws, the gray whales will continue to travel up and down the Eastern Pacific Ocean in the future.

Using Time Shifts and Tense

1. The example paragraph below is mainly about the present. Notice how the tenses change and how time words show these changes.

(1) **These days** *many of the teachers at our high school* **are struggling** *to control their classes. (2) Teachers* **feel** *that their students* **don't respect** *them. (3) They* **say** *this lack of respect* **makes** *them less successful as teachers. (4) What* **is happening** *in our classrooms? (5)* **Several months ago**, *a school committee* **asked** *students to describe successful teachers. (6) The students' responses* **were** *very interesting. (7) Students* **emphasized** *the importance of classroom control and challenging lessons. (8) These responses* **show** *that teachers* **need** *to use discipline in their classrooms and assign more difficult work. (9) We* **have to solve** *these problems* **now** *so that they* **will not become** *worse* **in the future**.

NOTE: This paragraph is mainly about the present situation in the school. However, sentences 5 through 7 switch to the past to talk about a situation from several months ago, and the second part of sentence 9 switches to the future.

2. The example paragraph below is mainly about the past. Notice how the tenses change and how time words show these changes.

(1) Students **say** *that they* **want** *discipline in the classrooms, but they* **do not** *always* **behave** *that way. (2) For example, a problem* **happened** *in our high school* **two months ago**. *(3) Some students* **injured** *a substitute teacher who* **had been** *unable to control the class. (4) The trouble* **began** *when several boys* **insulted** *the teacher and* **ended** *when the principal and security* **arrived**. *(5)* **Afterward**, *the boys* **didn't apologize** *for what they* **had done**. *(6) The principal* **suspended** *them for the* **rest of the year**. *(7) Unfortunately,* **in recent years** *this type of behavior* **has become** *more common.*

NOTE: This paragraph is mainly about an incident that happened two months ago. However, sentence 1 uses the present to introduce this example and sentence 7 switches to the present to show this type of behavior is common now and has been for a few years.

Choosing Tenses and Time Words

1. Use the correct tense for the time you are writing about. Make sure the tenses you choose work well together. Compare statements (A) and (B). Statement (A) shifts from the present to the past to the future, and statement (B) is all about the past.

> *(A) I'm tired today because I didn't sleep much last night. I'll go to bed*
>   simple present   simple past   future
>
> *early tonight.*

> *(B) I was tired yesterday because I hadn't slept much the night before, so I*
>   simple past   past perfect
>
>   *went to bed early last night.*
>   simple past

2. Use time words that are correct for the time frame that you are writing about.

Present time words/phrases: *today, (right) now, at the present, currently* (see Chapter 1)

> *My family lives in California now.*

Past time words/phrases: *yesterday, last night/week/month/year, ago* (see Chapter 2)

> *The prime minister spoke to parliament last night.*

Future time words/phrases: *tomorrow, next week/month/year, in the future* (see Chapter 4)

> *We will have our study group meeting tomorrow.*

3. Use time words to signal shifts in time. This helps readers follow your writing.

> *I saw a doctor last month, and now I'm feeling much better.*

> *Last year the government placed ten animals on the endangered species list. This list has grown longer in recent years.*

WRITING TIP

In all of your writing, check for correct time shifts by underlining time expressions and making sure they correspond to the verb tenses that you use in each sentence.

EDITING PRACTICE

1. *Put a check (✓) next to the sentences that use tenses and time words correctly. Correct the sentences that have errors.*

_____ **1.** His health has improved since he comes home from the hospital last

       month.

_____ **2.** The Martins are living in Australia now and will move to New Zealand

       later this year.

_____ **3.** May's father hasn't seen the grades that she receives on her last grade

       report.

_____ **4.** At first we only studied grammar and vocabulary, but now we are

writing paragraphs.

_____ **5.** In prehistoric times, men hunted for food and women prepare it.

_____ **6.** In many countries, government officials have many benefits, but the

citizens did not.

_____ **7.** In the next century, technology will be better than it is now.

_____ **8.** I had a headache for two hours; I'm going to take some aspirin.

_____ **9.** Nowadays most Americans did not remember the reasons for Memorial

Day, which they celebrate every May.

_____ **10.** The second grade students visited the school's garden last week, and

now they are learning about the plants that they saw.

_____ **11.** Joy and Joe are going to buy the old house that is on the corner.

_____ **12.** Sunny finishes only part of the exam before the teacher collected it.

2. _In the following paragraph, the underlined verbs are not correct. Write the correct verb form above each underlined verb._

I am going to visit my grandfather's house soon. I have not seen it in ten

years. However, I <u>knew</u> that it hasn't changed at all. Grandfather's house sits
       1

on the corner of a small street and has a large front gate with several trees

that are growing near it. The front door is bright red and <u>had</u> a window in
                              2

the middle of it. A high fence <u>surrounded</u> the house. In the front courtyard,
              3

beautiful flowers <u>grew</u> in many pots. Whenever I see those kinds of flowers
         4

today, they remind me of the happy times I <u>spend</u> at the house as a child.
              5

Ten years ago I <u>live</u> in the town near my grandfather's, and my father <u>takes</u>
     6   7

me to visit him almost every weekend. When we got there, we <u>enter</u> the
              8

house through the side door before my grandfather knew we <u>are</u> there. We
            9

always surprised him. I still <u>remembered</u> those times well. They are special
         10

memories that I will keep forever.

3. *Read the following essay. Complete the essay with the simple present, simple past, or future form of each verb. Use the time words to help you make the best choices.*

Years ago when I _____ in high school, I
                    1. be

_____ with the marching band every morning on the
   2. practice

football field at seven o'clock. The band had to finish practice by 8:00 A.M.

because the gardeners _____ to water the field, and we
                 3. begin

_____ to get wet! While we were practicing, the other
  4. want, not

students _____ to arrive at school. This
          5. start

_____ still my strongest high school memory because
   6. be

band practice _____ the best part of my four years at
        7. be

University High School. I _____ playing in the band, and I
           8. love

_____ so many good friends. We _____
   9. make   **10. be**

still good friends today. I _____ that we
           11. hope

_____ friends forever.
 12. remain

Today, University High _____ the largest high school
         13. be

in town with over 3,500 students. The campus _____
                 14. have

many large two-story buildings, a new football field, gymnasium, and

auditorium, and several computer and science labs. The school now

_____ many blocks in the downtown area. The area is
  15. cover

growing very fast, so the school _____ nearly 4,000
             16. have

students next year. It isn't the same school I _____ to all
              17. go

those years ago, but it still _____ many happy memories
          18. hold

for me.

4. *The following paragraph has ten errors in the use of tense. Use the time words to help you find and correct the errors.*

Many people are *now* adopting children who are five years or older from poor countries that cannot care for their orphans. *In the past,* I always plan to adopt an infant. I *still* thought that adopting an orphan or mistreated child is a wonderful thing to do; however, I am *now* learning that it is difficult to raise an orphaned child. *A few months ago,* my neighbors adopted a seven-year-old boy. *Before* I met their new son, I believe he was going to be happy with kind and loving parents. However, *now* I am not so certain. He doesn't understand love because he never receives love *in the first few years of his life. By the time he was five,* he develops behaviors that were normal for a child who did not have loving parents. In his *current* loving family, these behaviors were not appropriate. The child is slowly adapting to his new environment, and in the *next few years* he becomes comfortable with his new family and surroundings. I *now* see the challenges that adopted children brought to families. I *still* believe children are wonderful, and they increased the joy in their parents' lives, but *sometimes* adoption led to problems.

WRITING TOPICS

Read the student's paragraph about a memorable event in the past. Underline at least five examples of time shifts. Notice that the paragraph includes a clear topic sentence, supporting sentences, and a concluding sentence. Use this paragraph as a model when you write about one of the topics below.

When I was twelve years old, my family moved from India to the United States. I have lived in the United States for six years, but the move is still the most memorable event in my life. First of all, I had to leave my friends who I had known for my whole life. I was feeling lonely for months after we arrived in the United States. I now have many good American friends, but it took a few years to feel comfortable with them. Besides friendships, I had to leave a very good school in India. I was in a private school for elite students while I was living in India, but I had to go to a public school in the United States. I have learned to accept the differences in the two schools over the past six years. I love the freedom in American schools but miss the discipline in Indian schools. Food is the last reason my move from India to the United States is still memorable. My mother had always cooked delicious traditional food in India, but this changed in the United States. My mother didn't have as much time and was not able to find the best ingredients in our town in the United States. Many more Indian markets and people have moved to our area in the past six years, so traditional Indian food is improving and will continue to get better. However, I remember missing the food so much when we first came to the United States. For these three important reasons, moving from India to the United States will always be the most memorable event in my life.

Choose one of the topics and write at least one paragraph. Think carefully about the present, past, and future time frames as you write. Use time words to signal time shifts. After you complete your first draft, concentrate on editing your work. Keep in mind the editing practice from this chapter.

1. Describe the most memorable event from your childhood or adolescence. Why was this event significant? How are you different today because of this event?

2. Do you think it is better for children to follow their parents' plan for their future or for children to follow their own plan? What plan did your parents have for you when you were a child or a younger student? Have you followed this plan so far? Will you follow this plan in the future? Why or why not?

Go to page 115 for more practice with time shifts and tense.

Count and Uncountable Nouns

GRAMMAR FOCUS

There are two main groups of nouns in English: countable nouns, which refer to things that can be counted, and uncountable nouns (sometimes called *noncount*), which refer to things that cannot be counted. There are several differences between the two groups in form and use. To write clearly, it is important for you to understand these differences. Notice how the count and uncountable nouns are used in the following sentences.

UNCOUNTABLE NOUN	**Jewelry** is expensive.
SINGULAR COUNT NOUN	A **jewel** is a diamond, ruby, emerald, or other precious stone.
PLURAL COUNT NOUN	**Rings** are a symbol of love.

Pretest

Check your understanding of count and uncountable nouns. Put a check (✓) next to the sentences that are correct.

_____ **1.** Please help me correct the grammars in my paragraph.

_____ **2.** The parks in our city are full of birds.

_____ **3.** Last night Lisa wrote a six-pages paper.

_____ **4.** My friends want to have four childrens.

_____ **5.** We have been to the museum four time.

_____ **6.** Did the traffics slow you down today?

_____ **7.** Our cat has a broken leg.

_____ **8.** Thiefs have broken into many houses on my block.

_____ **9.** Would you rather plant flowers or fruit in the garden?

_____ **10.** I prefer taking a vacations on my birthday rather than receiving gifts.

GRAMMAR IN CONTEXT

Read the paragraph. Notice how count and uncountable nouns are used. Some of the nouns are underlined. Label the underlined nouns with C if they are count nouns and U if they are uncountable nouns.

People have become more worried about the environment recently. Pollution has been a problem for many decades, but global warming is now a big concern. Scientists are telling us that global warning can cause many environmental disasters such as hurricanes, droughts, and rising ocean levels. Because of these threats, people are beginning to change their habits. Bicycles are popular and so are hybrid cars because they burn less fuel than regular cars. Recycling is very common, and buying local food is also popular. There are many ways to help keep the environment clean for future generations.

Count Nouns

1. Count nouns are nouns that you can count separately (e.g., *car: a car, one car, two cars,* etc.) Because count nouns can be counted, they have singular and plural forms (e.g., *car* and *cars*). Singular count nouns use singular verb forms, and plural count nouns use plural verb forms.

2. Regular plurals are generally formed by adding *–s.*

    student — students

    book   — books

3. Spelling changes are required in some cases.

If a noun ends in *–ch, –sh, –ss,* or *–x,* add *–es.*

    patch — patches

    class   — classes

If a noun ends in a consonant + *–y,* change *–y* to *–i* and add *–es.*

    baby   — babies

    lady   — ladies

If a noun ends in *–f* or *–fe,* change the *–f* or *–fe* to *–v* and add *–es.*

    leaf   — leaves

    wife   — wives

If a noun ends in a vowel + *–o,* add *–s.*

    radio — radios

If a noun ends in a *consonant + –o,* add *–es.*

    tomato — tomatoes

4. Some plural count nouns are irregular; they do not use the *–s* ending.

SINGULAR	PLURAL
child	children
woman	women
person	people
foot	feet
phenomenon	phenomena

WRITING TIP

When you use a noun for the first time, refer to a dictionary if you are unsure of its plural form.

5. If a noun is used to modify another noun (if it is used as an adjective), it is always singular.

We have to read a **seven-chapter** *book in English.*

The firemen ran up a **ten-story** *building during the fire.*

Self Check 1
Circle the correct form of the noun.

1. The class had to write a (five-paragraph / five-paragraphs) paper.

2. The lecture was given by two (womans / women).

3. We visited three (cities / citys) in Spain.

4. The soccer team had two (matchs / matches) last week.

5. The books are on the (shelfs / shelves) in the living room.

Uncountable Nouns

1. Uncountable nouns are things that you cannot count separately. For example, in English you can say *honesty*, but you can't say *honesties*. Because these nouns cannot be counted, they generally cannot be plural.

WRITING TIP

Languages differ in whether a noun is considered count or uncountable. If you are not sure whether a noun is count or uncountable in English, look it up in your dictionary. An ESL dictionary such as the *Longman Dictionary of American English* will indicate whether nouns are count (C) or uncountable (U).

2. Many uncountable nouns fit into categories. Here are some examples:

Foods: *bread, cheese, meat, sugar*

Liquids: *coffee, gasoline, milk, paint, water, wine*

Solids: *glass, ice, paper, wood*

Gases: *air, oxygen, smog*

Particles: *dust, sand, sugar, salt*

Natural phenomena: *light, rain, thunder, weather*

Groups of similar items: *clothing, equipment, furniture, jewelry, junk, luggage, mail, makeup, money, stuff, traffic, vocabulary*

Abstract ideas: *advice, anger, beauty, employment, enjoyment, freedom, fun, hate, honesty, information, intelligence, knowledge, love, luck, news, patience, research, sadness, work*

Activities: *(gerunds) reading, swimming, writing*

Fields of study: *chemistry, literature, physics, psychology, mathematics, economics*

3. If the subject of the sentence is an uncountable noun, use a singular verb.

Good **luck comes** *in many forms.*

Smog is *a problem for the environment.*

NOTE: Even when an uncountable noun ends in *–s*, use a singular verb.

Physics is *my favorite subject.*

4. The articles *a/an* cannot be used with uncountable nouns.

I'm going to ask my uncle for advice.

                   not

I'm going to ask my uncle for an advice.

Self Check 2

The following sentences have errors involving uncountable nouns. Find and correct the errors.

1. My friends and I drink coffees together every morning.

2. I found some good informations about Shakespeare on the Internet.

3. We learned new vocabularies last week.

4. The clothing at the outdoor market are usually very inexpensive.

5. The school term was almost over, and the students were looking forward to their freedoms.

WRITING TIP

Edit your essay by reading it backwards from the last paragraph to the first. By reading the paragraphs out of the expected order, you may notice errors that you don't see when you read the essay in the usual way.

EDITING PRACTICE

1. *Put a check (✓) next to the sentences that use count and uncountable nouns correctly. Correct the sentences that have errors.*

_____ **1.** We sold all of our furniture at a garage sale.

_____ **2.** Jeanne's boss makes her do a lot of works.

_____ **3.** The research took a lot of time.

_____ **4.** I would like a bread and a piece of cheese.

_____ **5.** In some families, the wifes work while the husbands stay at home.

_____ **6.** My daughter lost two baby tooths last week.

_____ **7.** World music is very popular.

_____ **8.** There was many cars on the road this morning.

_____ **9.** I need to buy two pounds of flour.

_____ **10.** Many old homes have ten-feet ceilings.

2. *In the following paragraph, the underlined nouns are not correct. Write the correct noun form above each underlined noun.*

When <u>peoples</u> make an oversimplified generalization, this statement is
₁

called a *stereotype*. Almost everyone is familiar with some stereotypes. For

example, athletes are dumb and student interested in computers are nerds are

two common <u>stereotype</u>. One of the best sources of stereotypes is the state of
₂

California. People say that everyone in California surfs, eats health food, and

is tan. They all have blond <u>hairs</u>, too. Although these <u>statement</u> may be
₃ ₄

funny, sometimes stereotypes are unkind and cause <u>angers</u>. Therefore, it is
₅

important to avoid using oversimplified <u>generalization</u>. <u>Informations</u> and
₆ ₇

<u>educations</u> are the best ways to avoid <u>stereotypings</u> and the problems it
₈ ₉

can cause.

3. *Read the following paragraph. Complete the paragraph with the nouns given. Make them plural or leave them unchanged when necessary.*

Many high school seniors receive presents for graduation. Some get

_____ or nice _____. I also considered
　　　　1. money　　　　　　　　　　　　2. jewelry

asking for one of these when I graduated from high school. However, after

listening to the _____ of my older friends and siblings, I
　　　　　　　　　　　3. advice

decided that I really wanted a vacation in Mexico for my graduation gift. I

wanted to visit all of my _____. _____
　　　　　　　　　　　　4. relative　　　　　　　　　　5. excitement

and _____ in a foreign country sounded like so much fun.
　　　　6. travel

I received some new _____ from my grandmother and the
　　　　　　　　　　　　7. luggage

airline and train _____ from my parents. I had a wonderful
　　　　　　　　　　8. ticket

summer in my native country and took many nice _____
　　　　　　　　　　　　　　　　　　　　　　9. trip

to the beach and surrounding areas. I hope to return many

_____ in the future. I am grateful to my family for this
　　　　10. time

wonderful graduation gift.

4. *The following paragraph has ten errors in the use of count and uncountable nouns. Find and correct the errors.*

While I was in high school, I had many good friend. Unfortunately,

some of my friends became more like enemies. During the first two years of

high school, my friends and I shared secrets and spent a lot of times together.

We had become friends in our ninth grade English class because we liked to

study grammars and read the 300-pages novels that the teacher assigned. The

problems started with two friends who didn't want to share anything—not

even clothings! They also began to tell lies to the rest of us. This experience

taught me the importances of honesties. Friends must always tell each other the truths. Now I have a new group of friend in college, and I hope these new

friendships will last forever. It is impossible for friends to avoid trouble all of

the time, but I know the pain of losing friends, so I will do the best I can to

keep my new group together for the rest of our lifes.

WRITING TOPICS

Read the student's paragraph about a person whom she likes to talk to for advice. Circle the countable nouns and underline the uncountable nouns. Notice that the paragraph includes a clear topic sentence, supporting sentences, and a concluding sentence. Use this paragraph as a model when you write about one of the topics below.

When people have problems in life, they often need to talk with a close friend or family member. This is true for me too. I talk to my cousin, Husna, whenever I have a problem. There are several reasons why Husna is a good person to talk to. First of all, Husna has good listening skills. Good listeners pay attention to a person's words and actions before they give advice. Husna listens and hears more than my words. She looks into my face and can see how I feel. Besides good listening skills, Husna has a lot of knowledge. Wisdom helps us understand a situation and find a good solution. Husna is older than I am, so she has knowledge and wisdom that I do not have yet. This makes her advice very good. Finally, Husna is fair and wants to understand all sides of a problem. Fairness is an important quality in giving advice. Understanding a situation from all points of view guarantees the best solution and everyone's happiness. It is easy for people to give advice, but the best solutions to problems come from people like Husna who have good listening skills and are knowledgeable and fair.

Choose one of the topics and write one paragraph. Use singular and plural count nouns as well as uncountable nouns. After you complete your first draft, concentrate on editing your work. Keep in mind the editing practice from this chapter.

1. What is your favorite food or recipe? How do you prepare it? What ingredients are needed to make it? What do you like the best about this food? Is it prepared for special occasions?

2. We all experience new and difficult situations in life that we need to talk about. When you have one of these situations, whom do you talk to? Why do you choose to talk to this person? Describe why this person or people make you feel comfortable talking about your problems.

Go to page 117 for more practice with count and uncountable nouns.

Articles and Other Determiners

GRAMMAR FOCUS

Determiners go before nouns. There are four kinds of determiners:

- articles (*a, an, the*)

- quantifiers (*a lot of, a few,* etc.)

- demonstrative adjectives (*this, that, these, those*)

- possessive adjectives (*my, your,* etc.)

ARTICLE	**The** train is late.
QUANTIFIER	I need **a few** minutes to finish.
DEMONSTRATIVE ADJECTIVE	I'm enrolled in **that** class.
POSSESSIVE ADJECTIVE	**My** friend is going to help me.

To use the correct determiner, you need to know whether the noun is countable or uncountable (see Chapter 6). You also need to know whether you are referring to a noun in general or to a specific noun.

Pretest

Check your understanding of articles and other determiners. Put a check (✓) next to the sentences that are correct.

_____ **1.** That is best book on the bestseller list.

_____ **2.** Do you want to go to a movie tonight? I don't care which one.

_____ **3.** How was a lecture yesterday in Dr. Hui's class?

_____ **4.** Her children left sand all over my house after they went to the beach.

_____ **5.** We have to return this books to the library.

_____ **6.** Sharon was so full that she didn't eat any dinner.

_____ **7.** Jan bought several new CDs yesterday.

_____ **8.** We didn't find much computers on sale.

_____ **9.** Caroline and Rich said they would take the bike ride later today.

_____ **10.** Dan recognized a little songs at the concert.

GRAMMAR IN CONTEXT

Notice how the following paragraph uses articles and other determiners. Circle one of each of the following: article, quantifier, demonstrative adjective, and possessive adjective. Underline the noun that each of these modifies.

Training for a marathon takes a lot of hard work and time. If you want to run a marathon, the first step is to learn about marathons. It is important to read books, magazines, and websites about training for a marathon. Joining a running club is also a good idea. The next step is to buy the correct shoes for your feet. It is also a good idea to keep a running log of your running times and distances. The log has many benefits, but one of them is increasing your motivation. Next you need to increase your running mileage each week while avoiding injuries. If as a future marathoner you follow these steps, your training and race should be successful.

Articles

A, An, and *The*

1. Use *a* or *an* (the indefinite article) with singular count nouns to express general meaning. Use *a* or *an* when the thing you are referring to is not specific and the reader does not know which particular thing you are referring to.

   *Shawn bought **a** book last night.* (We don't know what book.)

   Use *a* before a noun beginning with a consonant sound (*a boy, a hunter, a university,* etc.).

   *His parents bought him **a** bicycle.*

   Use *an* before a noun beginning with a vowel sound (*an apple, an honor,* etc.).

   *You should bring **an** umbrella.*

   A or *an* usually cannot be used with an uncountable noun.

   Work gives us satisfaction and helps us earn money.

   not

   A work gives us a satisfaction and helps us earn a money.

   A singular count noun is always preceded by *a/an, the,* or another determiner (see page 48).

   *I ate **an/the/your** apple.*

   not

   I ate apple.

> ### WRITING TIP
>
> Highlight all singular count nouns in your essay. Make sure each of these has an article or another determiner preceding it.

2. No article (also known as Ø or *zero article*) is used with plural count nouns and uncountable nouns to express a general meaning.

> **Movies** *are a popular type of entertainment.*

> *Most people think that* **honesty** *is important.*

Generally, do not use an article with names of people, places, and things (also called *proper nouns*). Sometimes, however, *the* is part of the name.

> *Luis is originally from Caracas, Venezuela, but he now lives in* **the** *United States.*

3. *The* (the definite article) can be used to express specific meaning with all three kinds of nouns—singular count, plural count, and uncountable. In this case, the reader knows which particular thing you are referring to.

> **The** *assignment in art history is interesting.* (We know which assignment it is.)

> **The** *door was locked.* (The door was previously mentioned or is the only door.)

> **The** *trains are often crowded at this time of day.* (We can assume which trains.)

> *He gave us* **the** *information that we needed.* (We needed specific information.)

4. Use the definite article *the* in the following cases:

- with superlatives (the best, the cheapest, the most, the least, etc.)

  > **The fastest** *runner finished the race in ten minutes.*

- with ordinal numbers (the first, the second, the third, etc.)

  > *They didn't understand* **the second** *question on the test.*

- with *same*

  > *Dora and I have* **the same** *hairstyle.*

  > *Soo Jin made* **the same** *mistakes as I did.*

5. In general, select *a/an* or no article when using a noun for the first time and *the* (or another determiner) every time afterward.

> *I put* **a** *book in your room.* (indefinite—what book?)

> **The** *book is on your desk.* (definite—the book I put in your room)

> *We saw* **a** *good movie last night.* **The** *movie was about space aliens.*

> *We bought furniture yesterday.* **The** *furniture will be delivered tomorrow.*

Summary of Article Usage

Use the diagram to help you decide which articles to use with nouns.

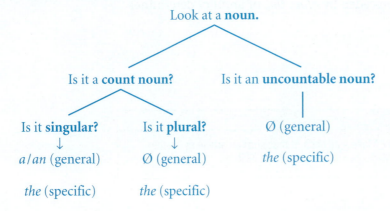

WRITING TIP

If you are having trouble deciding which article to use, refer to the diagram for help.

Self Check 1

Correct the errors involving articles.

1. My sister saw the good television show last night.

2. The class took an exam yesterday. An exam was hard.

3. There were very few scientists who had intelligence to understand Albert Einstein's work.

4. Parents teach their children about the life.

5. I think I answered last question incorrectly.

Other Determiners

Quantifiers

1. Use quantifiers before nouns to indicate an amount or number.

   *We brought **two** books and **several** magazines.*

2. Quantifiers that can be used with plural count nouns include the following:

| a few | a lot of/lots of | few | many | several | some |

   *Vy had **several** questions about the article she read.*

   Note the difference between the use of *few* and *a few:*

   Few *people came to the party. (*Meaning: We expected more people. Not very many people came to the party.)

   A few *people stayed late. (*Meaning: A small number of people stayed late.)

3. Quantifiers that can be used with uncountable nouns include the following:

| a little | a lot of/lots of | little | much | some |

   *The children didn't get **much** candy for Halloween.*

   Note the difference between the use of *little* and *a little:*

   *He gave me **little** help. (*Meaning: He didn't give me enough, or very much, help.)

   *He gave me **a little** help. (*Meaning: He gave me some, or a small amount of, help. It may have been enough help.)

4. *Some* is often replaced by *any* in questions and negative statements.

   *Did you have **any** problems with the assignment?*

   *No, I didn't have **any** problems. / Yes, I had **some** problems.*

5. *Much* is often used with uncountable nouns in questions and negative statements. It is unusual in affirmative statements. Use *a lot (of)* instead of *much* in affirmative statements.

> *Did you get* **much** *sleep last night?*

> *No, I didn't get* **much** *sleep. / Yes, I got* **a lot of** *sleep.*

6. *Each* and *every* are followed by singular count nouns + singular verbs.

> **Every student** *meets with an adviser once a year.*

> **Each university** *charges a different amount for room and board.*

Each of and *one of* + *the* are followed by a plural count noun. The verb remains singular.

> **Each of the students** *plans to take the test.*

> **One of the students** *isn't finished yet.*

Demonstrative Adjectives

Use the demonstrative adjectives *this* and *that* with singular count nouns and with uncountable nouns. Use *these* and *those* with plural count nouns.

> **This test** *is the hardest so far.*

> **That furniture** *looks beautiful in your house.*

> **These classes** *are at the introductory level.*

> *Did you pay a lot of money for* **those shoes**?

Possessive Adjectives

The following are the possessive adjectives:

her	his	its	my	our	their	your

Use possessive adjectives before a noun. They can be used with any kind of noun.

> **My parents** *live in Venezuela.*

> *We need to include* **their information** *in the report.*

NOTE: Do not confuse the possessive adjective *its* with *it's*, the contraction of *it is*.

> **Its** *writing program is very well known.* **It's** [it is] *among the best in the country.*

> Don't confuse the possessive adjective *their* with *there* or *they're (they are)*.

> **There** *are a lot of their newspapers in the trash.* **They're** [they are] *for recycling.*

Another and *Other*

1. Use *another* with singular count nouns. It means "one in addition to the one(s) already mentioned."

> *My older brother lives in Los Angeles, and I have* **another brother** *living in New York.*

2. Use *other* with plural count nouns and with uncountable nouns. It means "more or several more in addition to the one(s) already mentioned."

> *I finished the class, and* **other students** *finished too.* (Meaning: some in addition to me but not all)

> *He did* **other research** *that is very interesting.*

3. Use *the other* with singular or plural count nouns. It means "the rest of a specific group."

> *I finished the class, and* **the other student** *finished too.* (There was only one other student in the class.)

> *I finished the class, and* **the other students** *finished too.* (All the students finished.)

Self Check 2

Correct the errors in the use of determiners.

1. The child took each toys from the toy box.

2. The teenagers didn't buy many clothing at the mall.

3. My hiking group didn't see some wildflowers on our nature walk.

4. Each of the test is worth 100 points.

5. Can I make an appointment on other day?

WRITING TIP

Do a search with your word processing software for specific words or expressions to check that you've used them correctly. For example, do a search for *a* and check that you use it only before general or first-mention singular count nouns that begin with a consonant sound.

EDITING PRACTICE

1. *Put a check (✓) next to the sentences that use articles and other determiners correctly. Correct the sentences that have errors.*

_____ **1.** Parisa hopes that she gets better grade on the next quiz.

_____ **2.** Their guests arrived a few weeks after the Thanksgiving.

_____ **3.** There wasn't much news today.

_____ **4.** We get homework in every classes.

_____ **5.** Each student has to do an oral presentation.

_____ **6.** These test is difficult for students who have recently started to learn

English.

_____ **7.** I completely understand the directions. I don't have some questions.

_____ **8.** Yolanda wants an ice in her drink.

_____ **9.** This author has just written other book that you should read.

_____ **10.** One of the teacher is giving us a test next week.

2. In the following paragraph, five of the underlined phrases have errors in the use of nouns and determiners. Write your corrections above each underlined phrase.

I am living with several roommates for <u>the first time</u>. Because of this, I
                                              1

now see that there are <u>morning personalities</u> and <u>night personalities</u>. There
                              2   3

are people who wake up without <u>alarm clock</u> at 7:00 A.M. and are ready to
                                      4

start the day with a smile. However, <u>the same people</u> are asleep by 10:00 P.M.
                                            5

Then there are others who have energy at 10:00 P.M. but don't get out of

bed until noon or later. Everyone has energy at different times of the day.

<u>Each roommates</u> in my house has a different body clock. Sometimes
      6

<u>these difference</u> can make living together <u>a problem</u>. We have had
      7   8

<u>a few disagreements</u> because of music, phones, and alarms going off at
      9

different times of the day and night. The most important lesson we have

learned is <u>the patience</u>. Patience and communication are the only ways we
              10

will be able to remain friends <u>this year</u>. By living with roommates, I have
                                    11

learned a lot about different lifestyles and sleeping preferences. It has really

opened <u>the eyes</u>!
          12

3. Read the following paragraph. Complete the paragraph with a, the, or Ø (no article).

Living in _____ new country is an adventure. There
                1. a / the / Ø

are so many different customs that one must learn. I experienced this when I

was _____ foreign exchange student for one year in
          2. a / the / Ø

_____ France. There were a lot of customs that were new
      3. a / the / Ø

and strange at first but became natural after _____ few
                                                    4. a / the / Ø

months. After returning to _____ United States, one of
                                  5. a / the / Ø

_____ most interesting things I noticed was the strange
6. a / the / Ø

customs here! I never thought about these customs before I lived overseas.

When I moved back home, _____ tipping was
7. a / the / Ø

_____ first custom that seemed strange. I also had to get
8. a / the / Ø

used to _____ traffic in my hometown. American drivers,
9. a / the / Ø

however, have _____ patience with traffic, whereas many
10. a / the / Ø

European drivers do not. An American custom that I now find sad is

_____ lack of extended family living in the same house
11. a / the / Ø

or nearby. I observed French family life while I was living in a French home.

_____ family that I lived with had grandparents in
12. a / the / Ø

_____ same house. The aunts, uncles, and cousins lived in
13. a / the / Ø

the same town. It was so nice to have family members close by.

_____ experiences that I had while living abroad taught
14. a / the / Ø

me about life in the United States as well as in Europe.

4. *The following paragraph has ten errors in the use of articles and other determiners. Find and correct the errors. There may be more than one way to correct some errors.*

Most of us have known much teachers throughout our lives. These

teachers may be schoolteachers, parents, relatives, friends, or neighbors.

Most students have been motivated by at least one teacher in their lives.

One important job of all teachers is building self-confidence, and other job

is motivating the students. Giving a praise is one of the most successful way

a teacher can help students learn. However, each teachers has his or her

own style for motivating students. Most "A" students are self-motivated.

They want to get good grades. Other students need a few encouragement from their teachers. Most students hope a teachers will speak kindly and give them guidance. My favorite elementary school teacher was excellent at motivating his students in a positive way, and he achieved very good results from his students with these method. Negative motivation may work with a few student, but most students work harder and more successfully with some positive reinforcement. As a college student, I still need positive feedback from my instructors. I believe people of all ages want an encouragement and praise while they are learning. The best teachers know this and use it to motivate their students.

WRITING TOPICS

Read the student's paragraph about her college campus. Think about why each underlined article or determiner is used. Notice that the paragraph includes a clear topic sentence, supporting sentences, and a concluding sentence. Use this paragraph as a model when you write a paragraph about one of the topics below.

Most college campuses have many good qualities, but I believe that my campus is special for several different reasons. First of all, the location of the campus makes it perfect for college students. It is in a small suburb near a medium-sized city. The small town has friendly people, a safe and clean environment, and a slow pace of life. There are few things in town to take students away from their schoolwork. However, city life is not very far away. In less than an hour, students can be at the theater, a concert, a museum, or other fun places that cities have. In addition to location, there are a lot of campus resources and organizations at my college. Students can get academic assistance with their studies from tutors, the writing center, the math lab, or the skill development center. These are just a few of the places where students can find help. The social organizations are one of the best parts of my campus. There are fraternities and sororities, athletic and academic clubs, many sporting events, and cultural festivals. During every week of the semester, a different social event happens. Another benefit of my college is its cultural diversity. International students from around the world come to this college. This cultural diversity makes classroom discussions interesting. Students can learn so much from other students who have different points of view. It also makes the campus festivals and social events unique. Students should consider many different qualities when they choose a college. The location, campus resources and organizations, and cultural diversity are the qualities that make my campus a wonderful place to study.

Choose one of the topics and write one paragraph. Use a variety of articles and other determiners. After you complete your first draft, concentrate on editing your work. Keep in mind the editing practice from this chapter.

1. What is your nickname or the nickname of someone you know? What does the nickname mean? How did you or this person acquire the nickname? Do you like it? What significance does it have to you, your friends, or family members?

2. Pretend your best friend is currently attending a different school. You would like to convince him or her to transfer to your school. Describe the school you are at now so that your friend will be interested in visiting or even transferring.

Go to page 118 for more practice with articles and other determiners.

8 Pronouns

GRAMMAR FOCUS

Pronouns, words like *I*, *him*, *it*, *our*, and *themselves*, take the place of nouns. They make writing less repetitive and link ideas within sentences and between paragraphs. Notice how the pronoun in the second sentence of each pair below agrees with the noun in the first sentence and helps join together the ideas within the two sentences.

> *Joanne and Howard bought a new tent.* **They** *are going camping.*

> *We sat next to Mr. and Mrs. Jackson.* **We** *had an interesting conversation with* **them**.

> *Grace and I have new shoes.* **Hers** *are more expensive than* **mine**.

	SUBJECT PRONOUNS	OBJECT PRONOUNS	POSSESSIVE PRONOUNS	REFLEXIVE PRONOUNS
Singular	I	me	mine	myself
	you	you	yours	yourself
	he	him	his	himself
	she	her	hers	herself
	it	it		itself
Plural	we	us	ours	ourselves
	you	you	yours	yourselves
	they	them	theirs	themselves

Pretest

Check your understanding of pronouns. Put a check (✓) next to the sentences that are correct.

_____ **1.** They left the class without you and I.

_____ **2.** My mother and me took an accounting class last year.

_____ **3.** Marvin and I flew to Frankfurt, but him and me did not sit together.

_____ **4.** Victor and Juan need to work on pronunciation, so they practice his pronunciation together.

_____ **5.** They are reading by themselves to increase their speed.

_____ **6.** I left my book at home. May I look at yours?

_____ **7.** These suitcases are not ours. Ours are already in the car.

_____ **8.** I loaned my notes to a classmate. I need to get them back from him soon.

_____ **9.** The bicycle trails are fantastic even though there is a lot of walking traffic on it.

_____ **10.** Your children can stay with me for the weekend.

GRAMMAR IN CONTEXT

Notice how the following paragraph uses pronouns to refer back to certain nouns. Some of the pronouns are underlined. Circle the noun that the pronoun refers to. The pronoun usually appears soon after the noun it refers to.

Because it is very expensive to keep prisoners in jail, many cities and states require that criminal offenders do community service. <u>This</u> is an alternative punishment to jail or sometimes in addition to <u>it</u>. Community service is for people who commit minor offenses. <u>These</u> might include traffic violations and littering, for example. If someone is caught committing one of these crimes, <u>he or she</u> might have to pick up trash, help the elderly, work at a local library, or help fire and police services. Community service helps communities save costs. However, <u>its</u> main benefit is to educate criminals about ethical behavior and train <u>them</u> to behave in responsible ways in the future.

Kinds of Pronouns

1. Use subject pronouns as the subjects of sentences.

> **You** _and_ **I** _should talk more often._
>
> _In the winter,_ **they** _love to ski._

2. Use object pronouns as the objects of verbs and of prepositions.

> _My professor likes_ **me** _because I work so hard in her class._
>
> _Mr. Liu gave the package to_ **him**_._

3. Use possessive pronouns in place of a possessive adjective + noun.

> _John's car is more expensive than_ **mine**_._ (my car)
>
> _Louisa received her copy in the mail yesterday. Did you receive_ **yours**_?_
> (your copy)

NOTE: Do not confuse possessive pronouns with possessive adjectives. A possessive adjective is always used with a noun; a possessive pronoun is always used alone. For more on possessive adjectives, see page 95.

4. Use reflexive pronouns instead of object pronouns when the object refers to the same person or thing as the subject.

> *He always tests* **himself** *before an exam.* (*himself* = He)

> not

> *He always tests* **him** *before an exam.* (*him* = another person)

5. The demonstrative pronouns are *this, that, these,* and *those.* They identify or point to nouns. A demonstrative pronoun must agree with the noun it refers to. *This* and *that* refer to singular nouns; *these* and *those* refer to plural nouns.

> *He got an A on his history paper.* **This** *was the best paper he wrote all year.*

> *Everyone enjoyed the fireworks and dancing.* **These** *were the best parts of the day.*

This and *that* can be used to refer to ideas, situations, or actions that were just mentioned. When you use them in this way, make sure readers know what they refer to.

> *The final exam will be difficult.* **This** *means we will have to study.* (*This* = the fact that the final will be difficult)

> *I took three exams last week.* **That** *was an exhausting experience.* (*That* = the fact that I took three exams last week)

> **NOTE:** Do not confuse demonstrative pronouns with demonstrative adjectives. A demonstrative adjective is always used with a noun; a demonstrative pronoun is always used alone. For more on demonstrative adjectives, see page 58.

6. Indefinite pronouns are formed by combining *every, some, any,* and *no* with *one, body,* or *thing* (e.g., *everyone, somebody, anybody, nothing*). Use them to refer to people and things in general or to unspecified people and things.

Use singular verbs for all indefinite pronouns.

> **Everything looks** *perfect.*

Pronouns and possessive adjectives that are used with indefinite pronouns must also be singular.

> **Everyone** *must learn these answers for* **himself.**

> or

> **Everyone** *must learn these answers for* **himself** *or* **herself.**

> **Anyone** *can give* **his** *or* **her** *opinion.*

7. *Another, others,* and *the other(s)* can be used as pronouns. They can also be used as determiners. (See Chapter 7 for more information on determiners.)

> *If you've finished that book, the library will lend you* **another.**

> *Some of the guests are here, but we're waiting for* **others** *to arrive.*

Circle the answer that completes the sentence correctly.

1. (Her and Jade / She and Jade) are going to take the subway.

2. The usher showed (Ken and I / Ken and me) to our seats.

3. Doris got three As this semester. (These are / This are) her best grades ever.

4. Everyone got (their / his or her) passport before boarding the plane.

5. If you like this novel, I'll loan you (other / another).

Using Pronouns

1. Choose pronouns carefully. Choose a subject pronoun, object pronoun, or reflexive pronoun as needed in the sentence.

   The car accident **injured** *(verb) Michelle and* **me** *(object pronoun for object of the verb).*

                              not

   The car accident injured Michelle and I.

                         or

   The car accident injured Michelle and myself.

2. Make the pronoun agree with the noun it replaces.

   The **banking industry** *is changing.* **It** *has to change because of new technology and laws. (It* = banking industry)

   Michelle *drives* **Gail and me** *to school every day.* **She** *picks* **us** *up in front of* **our** *house. (She* = Michelle; *us* and *our* = Gail and me)

3. In some cases a pronoun refers to either a male or a female. Traditionally, masculine pronouns *(he, him, his)* have been used. However, it is now common to use both masculine and feminine pronouns *(he or she, him or her,* etc.).

   Before a **teacher** *begins a class,* **he** *does a lot of preparation.* (traditional)

   Before a **teacher** *begins a class,* **he or she** *does a lot of preparation.* (now common)

   Books can be used during the exam, so **each student** *should bring* **his** *on the day of the exam.* (traditional)

   Books can be used during the exam, so **each student** *should bring* **his or hers** *on the day of the exam.* (now common)

WRITING TIP

Using only masculine pronouns excludes females, but repeating *he or she* can become awkward. To avoid this problem, consider using the plural form of the noun and pronoun.

Before **teachers** begin a class, **they** do a lot of preparation.

Books can be used during the exam, so **students** should bring **theirs** on the day of the exam.

EDITING PRACTICE

1. *Put a check (✓) next to the sentences that use pronouns correctly. Correct the sentences that have errors. Be sure to use correct subject-verb agreement if you change a pronoun.*

_____ **1.** Ms. Sharpe will discuss the project with Donna and I.

_____ **2.** Encouraging someone to smoke when they don't want to is wrong.

_____ **3.** My father asked Sam to do many household chores, but Sam couldn't do it immediately.

_____ **4.** Two tennis players hurt themselves when they were practicing for the tournament.

_____ **5.** Theresa has so much homework, but she doesn't have time to do them.

_____ **6.** When a musician gives a concert, he or she must practice before the performance.

_____ **7.** Each girl on the basketball team has their strengths.

_____ **8.** Farid moved to the United States. These were very good for his career.

_____ **9.** Bob and I just got new running shoes. His are larger than mine.

_____ **10.** Me and Paulo are going on vacation.

2. *In the following paragraph, the underlined pronouns are not correct. Write the correct pronoun form above each underlined pronoun. Be sure to use correct subject-verb agreement if you change a pronoun.*

The Fourth of July is one of the most popular holidays in the United States. On this day Americans celebrate <u>his or her</u> independence. A typical
₁
Fourth of July includes spending time with family and friends, having picnics, and watching fireworks. Most Americans do not spend this day by <u>theirselves</u>. Many communities celebrate with a pancake breakfast and a
₂
parade in the morning. Later in the afternoon, some families have parties in their backyards or at the beach. Barbecues are popular too, because <u>it</u>
₃
is casual, and the food is so delicious that both adults and children enjoy <u>them</u>. If a person watches television or listens to the radio on the Fourth,
₄

they will see or hear many patriotic shows. After the sun sets, it is time for
5

the fireworks. Even though these are illegal in many places, people still play

with it. Many communities have professional fireworks shows so that a child
6

doesn't hurt themselves playing with it. Besides these festivities, everyone
7   8

has to wear red, white, and blue or him or her looks out of place. These
9

colors are almost required on the Fourth. Even though there are so many fun

holidays in the United States, many people consider the Fourth of July their

favorite compared to another.
10

3. *Read the following paragraph. Complete the paragraph with the correct
pronoun or possessive adjective.*

In my opinion, communism is a terrible system of government. My

family and _____ lived under _____
              1. I / me / myself   **2. them / its / it**

during my childhood. A communist government hurts people more than it

helps _____. Communism is supposed to make people
      3. them / theirs / themselves

equal, but _____ does almost the opposite. The people
           4. we / they / it

are supposed to own all the property; however, the people work for the

government rather than for _____. A man could work
             5. himself / theirselves / themselves

twelve hours a day and still not have enough money to support

_____ family. People also do not have freedom of speech.
     6. his / your / their

No one is allowed to say what _____ thinks. Many people
               7. they / he or she / we

do not practice religion because _____ goes against
               8. these / those / this

communism. In my opinion, communism and _____ laws
               9. our / their / its

have hurt many countries. Sadly, these are only some of the results of

communism. There are _____.
     10. another / others / the other

4. *The following essay has ten errors in the use of pronouns. Find and correct the errors. Be sure to check for subject–verb agreement if you change a pronoun.*

There are several theories that describe immigrant countries such as the United States, Australia, and Canada. One theory is the Salad Bowl Theory. It claims that all immigrants should keep his or her individuality but can also add to the main culture. These society looks like one large salad with many different ingredients. Large cities are good examples of the theory. These cities have different ethnic communities that live by itself. However, these communities also contribute to the diversity of their cities. Every neighborhood has their own characteristics but lives together as one large community or salad.

The Melting Pot Theory describes another way for different cultures to live together. This theory states that when an immigrant comes to a new country, they should leave their old culture and traditions at home. In other words, immigrants must "melt" into the main culture. In the past, many immigrant groups gave up his or her culture and language, while today many groups do the opposite and try not to lose his.

Although this is two common theories, there is another. Perhaps first-generation immigrants follow the Salad Bowl Theory while his or her children and grandchildren begin to melt into the main culture. A combination of the two theories might be the most accurate way to describe immigrant societies.

WRITING TOPICS

Read the student's paragraph about a book. Circle all of the pronouns and possessive adjectives in the paragraph. The paragraph includes a clear topic sentence, supporting sentences, and a concluding sentence. Use this paragraph as a model when you write a paragraph about one of the topics below.

I definitely want to recommend the book *Rain Man* by Leonore Fleischer. This is a very good book for several reasons. First of all, autism is a mysterious disability and *Rain Man* describes it well. I now feel more compassion for children who have it because of the character Raymond in the novel. Raymond helped me know that there is a real person behind the disability. *Rain Man* also showed me real life in the United States. Americans put people in homes when they get old or have a disability. This book helped me understand the reasons people might do this. I still do not agree with it, but I can see why some Americans do. This knowledge will help me live in this country more easily. Finally, *Rain Man* has many useful vocabulary words. The novel has some informal conversations between Raymond and Charlie. The everyday vocabulary and usage in the novel seem very natural and easy to use. I like to know how people really talk because it helps me improve my conversation. There are many other reasons that *Rain Man* is an excellent novel, but these are the three most important reasons.

Choose one of the topics and write one paragraph. Use as many different pronouns as possible. After you complete your first draft, concentrate on editing your work. Keep in mind the editing practice from this chapter.

1. Briefly summarize a movie or book you recently saw or read. Who were the main characters? What did they do? Why did you like or dislike the movie or book? Will you recommend it to your friends? Why or why not?

2. What are the characteristics of a good teacher? How do good teachers help create better students or people? To support your ideas, you can describe the best teacher you have ever had and the characteristics that made him or her a good teacher.

Go to page 120 for more practice with pronouns.

9 Modals

GRAMMAR FOCUS

Modals are auxiliary verbs. They are used with main verbs to give advice and to express ideas such as ability, necessity, or possibility. Examples of modals are *can, might,* and *should.* Most modals have more than one meaning. For example, *can* is used for possibility, ability, and permission.

Phrasal modals are expressions with meanings similar to those of modal auxiliaries. They include expressions like *be able to, be supposed to,* and *have to.* Notice how the modals in the following sentences change the meaning of each sentence even though everything else in the sentence remains the same.

POSSIBILITY	Our study group **may** meet in the library today.
ADVICE	Our study group **should** meet in the library today.
NECESSITY	Our study group **has to** meet in the library today.

Pretest

Check your understanding of modals. Put a check (✓) next to the sentences that are correct.

_____ **1.** Jim should gives his mother a nice gift on Mother's Day.

_____ **2.** Last semester I had to write three essays in one night.

_____ **3.** Mozart was a child prodigy; he can play the piano at a very young age.

_____ **4.** If you want a good grade, you can study tonight.

_____ **5.** This book may be the best one that I have ever read.

_____ **6.** The law says that people must not smoke on airplanes.

_____ **7.** I think we are suppose to turn right on Central Avenue.

_____ **8.** It snowed a lot, so we not able to drive home last night.

_____ **9.** Lonnie is very sick. She had better see a doctor soon.

_____ **10.** I want to offer you a job. I may only afford to pay minimum wage.

GRAMMAR IN CONTEXT

Notice how modals are used in the following paragraph. Circle each modal and verb combination. Think about the meaning of each modal.

The number of people over eighty years old is growing. Some predictions say that by 2050 there will be 4 million people over eighty in the world. It is exciting that so many people could live longer and healthier lives. However, a large elderly population may create some problems. As the number of eighty-year-olds increases, the population will increase. Environmental problems could occur because of the larger population. As a result, there might not be enough food and water for everyone. As some scientists work on lengthening our lives, other scientists should find solutions to the problems that longer lives could create.

Table 1. **Dynamics of Population Aging in the Modern World**

Observed and Forecasted Percentages of the Elderly (65+ years) in Selected Areas, Regions, and Countries of the World: 1950, 2000, and 2050

MAJOR AREA, REGION, OR COUNTRY	1950	2000	2050
World	5.2%	6.9%	19.3%
Africa	3.2%	3.3%	6.9%
Latin America and the Caribbean	3.7%	5.4%	16.9%
China	4.5%	6.9%	22.7%
India	3.3%	5.0%	14.8%
Japan	4.9%	17.2%	36.4%
Europe	8.2%	14.7%	29.2%
Italy	8.3%	18.1%	35.9%
Germany	9.7%	16.4%	31.0%
Sweden	10.3%	17.4%	30.4%
U.S.A.	8.3%	12.3%	21.1%

Source: United Nations 2001 (http://longevity-science.org/Population_Aging.htm)

Forming Modals

Present and Future Time

1. Modal auxiliaries have only one form. Use a modal + the base form of the verb. The base form of the verb is used with all subjects. Do not add –s to the base form for third-person singular subjects. For negative statements, put *not* after the modal.

	AFFIRMATIVE			NEGATIVE	
	MODAL + BASE FORM OF VERB			**MODAL + *NOT* + BASE FORM OF VERB**	
I	can		I	cannot*	
	could			could not	
	will			will not	
You	would		You	would not	
He, She, It	should	+ eat	He, She, It	should not**	+ eat
We	ought to		We		
You	may		You	may not	
	might			might not	
They	must		They	must not	
	had better			had better not	

*Cannot *is written as one word.*

**Americans do not usually use the negative of* ought to. *Use* should not *instead.*

He **may need** more time to finish his paper.

         not

He may needs more time to finish his paper.

Mario **had better not drive** too fast because there are many policemen nearby.

         not

Mario had not better drive too fast because there are many policemen nearby.

2. Although modals do not change form with different subjects, phrasal modals with *be* and *have* do change form to agree with the subject.

I **am supposed to practice** *today.*

Michael **has to help** *his parents move.*

John and Kim **are not able to do** *their homework this afternoon.*

3. To form questions with modals, do not use the *do* auxiliary. The modal functions as *do* or *does* in questions.

> **Can** *Hiro* **speak** *Japanese and English?*

> **May** *I* **take** *your picture?*

4. To form questions and negatives with *have to*, use *do, does, do not,* or *does not*.

> *What* **do** *we* **have to do** *for homework?*

> **Does** *he* **have to make** *an appointment?*

> *We* **don't have to finish** *our essay until Friday.*

> *Maria* **doesn't have to work** *today.*

Past Time

The following are the past forms for some modals and phrasal modals.

PRESENT	PAST
can	could
have to/has to	had to
am/is/are/able to	was/were able to
am/is/are supposed to	was/were supposed to

> *When Marina was a child, she* **could play** *the violin well.*

> *We* **had to call** *the police after the car accident.*

> *The plane* **wasn't able to take off** *because of the snowstorm.*

> *We* **were supposed to call** *home as soon as we arrived.*

Self Check 1

Circle the correct form of the modal.

1. Financial aid (can helps / can help) students continue their education.

2. Desert communities (has to / have to) conserve water.

3. You (should study not / should not study) with the television on.

4. Robert (have to / has to) prepare a presentation.

5. (Does Pat have / Has Pat) to study tonight?

Using Modals

MEANING	PRESENT AND FUTURE	PAST
Showing ability	can	could
	am/is/are able to	was/were able to
	*She **can** play the piano very well.*	*She **could** play the piano very well when she was younger.*
Making requests	can	
	could	
	would	
	***Would** you edit my essay?*	
Showing possibility	can	
	may	
	might	
	could	
	*Martina **might** take an art class.*	
Showing near certainty (deduction)	must	must have
	*His office door is locked; he **must** not be here today.*	*His car is not here; he **must have** left already.*
Asking for and giving permission	can	
	could	
	may	
	*(A) **May** I borrow this book?* *(B) Sure you **can**.*	
Showing necessity	must	
	has/have to	had to
	*They **must** arrive by 10:15 A.M.* *She **has to** buy a birthday present for her sister.*	
Showing prohibition	must not	
	cannot	
	*Students **cannot** talk during the exam.*	
Showing lack of necessity	do/does not + have to	did not have to
	*You **don't have to** finish the essay until next week.*	*We **did not have to** revise the final essay.*
Giving strong advice or warning	had better (not)	
	*You **had better not** wait to start studying for the final exam.*	

MEANING	PRESENT AND FUTURE	PAST
Making suggestions/giving advice	am/is/are supposed to	was supposed to
	should	
	ought to	
	can	
	could	
	We **should** *visit our professor during office hours.* *You* **ought to** *ask the professor for help if you don't understand the reading.*	*He* **was supposed to** *cook dinner last night.*

Self Check 2

Circle the answer that completes the sentence correctly.

1. The instructor says that we (must / might) not talk during the exam.

2. You (had better / had better not) turn in the assignment late or you'll get a bad grade.

3. Arturo (doesn't have to / must not) take the final exam; he can write a research paper instead.

4. Cats (may / can) climb trees and see in the dark.

5. The doors are locked, and the windows are closed; they (must / should) be out of town.

WRITING TIP

Read your essay out loud several times. Sometimes it's easy to hear grammar errors that you miss during silent reading.

EDITING PRACTICE

1. *Put a check (✓) next to the sentences that use modals correctly. Correct the sentences that have errors.*

_____ **1.** You're very busy right now, so you are not supposed to do the dishes.

_____ **2.** Diane better study harder to pass the test.

_____ **3.** Ava ought to finish her paper tonight.

_____ **4.** Mr. Pelly can calls Yi-Ting on her cell phone.

_____ **5.** Would you offer my son a job?

_____ **6.** You must not to call 911 unless it is an emergency.

_____ **7.** When we arrived at the airport, we cannot find parking.

_____ **8.** The Nelson family is not able to afford a vacation this year.

_____ **9.** John could not study last night because he has to work.

_____ **10.** Drivers should not talk on the phone and drive at the same time.

_____ **11.** Christina and Kenneth studied all night. They must be tired today.

2. *In the following paragraph, seven of the underlined modal and verb combinations are not correct. Find and correct the errors.*

There are many differences between schools in foreign countries and in the United States. One difference between Asian and American schools is showing respect. In Asian schools, the students <u>must stand</u> when the teacher

1

enters the classroom. When I studied in an Asian school, I <u>have to bow</u> to

2

my teachers. To most Americans, this respect <u>must to look</u> strange, and this

3

behavior <u>may seems</u> unusual. Another difference is parents and teachers

4

force children to study in Asia. They believe children <u>can not study</u> well

5

without their elders' help. A final difference is the punishment in Eastern schools. In my primary school, when students didn't work hard, teachers

<u>were supposed to slap</u> them on the hand. When my family and I came to the

6

United States, we <u>has to change</u> to a very different type of education. Now I

7

<u>could study</u> without punishment or force from my parents and teachers. The

8

two styles of education come from each country's history and culture. In my

opinion, the best educational style <u>had better be</u> a combination of Eastern

9

and Western.

3. *Underline the modals in the following sentences. In your own words, write the meaning of each sentence in the blank. Use a different modal to explain the meaning or explain the meaning without using a modal.*

Example:

You <u>have to</u> put the stamp in the upper right corner of the envelope.

Meaning: It is necessary <u>to put the stamp in the upper right corner of the envelope.</u>

1. Arman, Isabel, and Ali may go out for dinner tonight.

Meaning: _____

2. We have to read the whole textbook this semester.

Meaning: _____

3. I should learn to speak a second language.

Meaning: _____

4. Many Italians can cook very well.

Meaning: _____

5. Marcus must learn to swim before he goes in the pool.

Meaning: _____

4. *Underline the ten modal and verb combinations used in this essay. Six have errors. Find and correct the errors. There may be more than one way to correct some errors.*

    History textbooks can be boring for many students to read. Because of this, historical novels must be a better way to learn history. The novel *Black Boy* by Richard Wright is a good example. It may helps readers understand African American history in the United States better than a history textbook can do this. In the novel, Richard Wright writes about his own life in the early 1900s. Richard's father leaves the family when Richard is a boy. Therefore, Richard might care for his home and family. Richard also have to be responsible. This is very difficult for a child. Even though he has many hardships, Richard is able to remain curious and interested in life. Later, Richard's mother has a stroke, so Richard must get help from his neighbors. Soon, Richard's grandmother comes to help the family. However, other relatives decide she is able not to take care of Richard's family very well. This story describes Richard's history and the hardships that many African Americans faced at that time. Unlike history lessons from a textbook, I can not forget the lessons from this novel.

WRITING TOPICS

Read the student's paragraph about social norms. Notice how the writer uses modal and verb combinations. The paragraph includes a clear topic sentence, supporting sentences, and a concluding sentence. Use this paragraph as a model when you write a paragraph about one of the topics below.

Social norms are rules or behaviors that people should follow. Children learn social norms by watching their parents, other adults, friends, and the media. A social norm for adults is not to cry when they become upset. Children can cry when they are little, but this behavior may not be accepted as they grow older. By watching adults, children learn that they should not cry when they get mad. Another example of a social norm is handshaking. Adults have to shake hands with other adults, but children generally do not shake hands. However, once children become teenagers, handshaking may be expected. By adulthood, people learn that they had better shake hands in certain situations. Not staring at strangers is another social norm that most adults must follow. Children can stare at strangers, but they are taught to stop staring as they get older. Children learn that they should not stare and staring might be rude. Like most social norms, the rules about crying, handshaking, and staring are not in a book, but adults know that they must follow these unwritten rules.

Choose one of the topics and write one paragraph. Use a variety of modals. After you complete your first draft, concentrate on editing your work. Keep in mind the editing practice from this chapter.

1. What should or must each of us do to make the world a better or safer place to live? What could each of us do to help reduce problems like racism, pollution, or violence?

2. The norms or rules that children must follow are different from the ones adults must follow. What are some rules that children must follow, and what are others that adults have to follow? What could you do as a child that you are not able to do now? What can you do now that you were not supposed to do as a child?

Go to page 122 for more practice with modals.

Sentence Structure and Punctuation

GRAMMAR FOCUS

Good sentence structure means being able to use simple, compound, and complex sentences well. Good writers must know how to use a variety of sentence types with the correct punctuation; good editors are able to locate and correct sentence structure errors such as fragments, comma splices, and run-on sentences. Notice how the following errors are easily fixed by using the correct sentence structure.

PROBLEM	INCORRECT	CORRECT
Fragment	Because it snowed last night.	Because it snowed last night, the schools are closed today.
Comma Splice	Spy movies are exciting, they have a lot of action.	Spy movies are exciting. They have a lot of action.
Run-On	Many classes were cancelled this semester Lena had to change her schedule.	Many classes were cancelled this semester, so Lena had to change her schedule.

Pretest

Check your understanding of sentence structure and punctuation. Put a check (✓) next to the sentences that are correct.

_____ **1.** Earthquakes happen.

_____ **2.** They put on the shelf.

_____ **3.** Her rent is due, she does not have any money.

_____ **4.** Before mobile phones were common, people used public pay phones.

_____ **5.** Dr. Wilkey is eighty-two years old he still works eight-hour days.

_____ **6.** Love the pizza in Chicago.

_____ **7.** A good paragraph has several parts. First, it has a topic sentence.

_____ **8.** On the last day of the month.

_____ **9.** Because Erika crashed her car she has to take the bus.

_____ **10.** Green tea is healthy but has a lot of caffeine.

GRAMMAR IN CONTEXT

Several different types of sentences are underlined in the following paragraph. In the margin, label the simple sentence SS, the compound sentence CS, the complex sentence CX, and the sentence that uses a transition T.

All good paragraphs have many of the same parts. <u>First, a paragraph must have a topic sentence.</u> The topic sentence introduces the topic of the paragraph and the controlling idea. Both are necessary in a well-written topic sentence. <u>After the topic sentence is written, the writer develops the major support sentences.</u> These sentences directly support the topic sentence. Most paragraphs have three major support sentences. Next, the writer has to develop the minor support sentences. <u>These sentences follow each major support sentence, and they give details to support the topic sentence.</u> There are usually six to nine minor support sentences. The last sentence of the paragraph is the concluding sentence. It is similar to the topic sentence but uses different words. <u>All well-written paragraphs have these four important parts.</u>

Forming Sentences

1. A simple sentence is the most basic sentence in English. It has a subject and a verb. Like all sentences, simple sentences always begin with a capital letter and end with a punctuation mark such as a period, question mark, or exclamation point.

> *Athletes work out.*

> *Students study.*

Although most sentences are longer than these two, all sentences have at least a subject and a verb. These sentences are also called independent clauses.

> *Athletes and coaches work out three times a day.*

> *Students study and socialize in the library.*

2. Verbs that are transitive must be followed by an object to form a complete sentence.

> *The people elected.* (incomplete sentence)

> *The people elected a new president.*

> *Professor Jones put on the desk.* (incomplete sentence)

> *Professor Jones put his book on the desk.*

WRITING TIP

A good dictionary will tell you if a verb is transitive or intransitive. If a verb is transitive it must be followed by an object. If it is intransitive, it does not need an object.

---

3. A compound sentence combines two simple sentences with a coordinating conjunction. The coordinating conjunctions are *for, and, nor, but, or, yet,* and *so*. The most frequently used coordinating conjunctions are *and, but, or,* and *so*. When you combine two sentences with a coordinating conjunction, use a comma after the first sentence.

> *Mr. Lyndon likes swimming,* **and** *his son likes surfing.* (*and* adds additional information)

> *Joe is shy,* **but** *he has many friends.* (*but* shows a contrast)

> *We might visit the museum,* **or** *we may see a movie.* (*or* gives a choice)

> *Jillian lives in an apartment,* **so** *she cannot have a pet.* (*so* shows a result)

If the two clauses have the same subject, leave out the second subject and the comma.

> *Mr. Lyndon likes swimming and has a swimming pool.*

> *Joe is shy but has many friends.*

> *We might visit the museum or see a movie.*

4. A complex sentence combines an independent clause and a dependent clause with a subordinating conjunction. There are many subordinating conjunctions. Some of the most frequently used subordinating conjunctions show time (*after, before, when, while, since*), reason or cause (*because, since*), and concession (*although, even though*).

> *The children played* **while** *their parents ate dinner.*

> *Tim and Marcy went to the doctor* **because** *Marcy felt sick.*

> *Brian bought a new car* **even though** *his old car was in good condition.*

When the sentence begins with a subordinating conjunction (or the dependent clause), use a comma before the independent clause.

> **While** *the parents ate dinner, their children played.*

> **Because** *Marcy felt sick, Tim and Marcy went to the doctor.*

> **Even though** *his old car was in good condition, Brian bought a new car.*

5. When there is a relationship between two simple sentences, the two simple sentences must be combined with a coordinating or subordinating conjunction. Without a conjunction, there is either a comma splice or a run-on sentence.

> *Jenna had twins last year,* **and** *her sister has twins too.* (compound sentence)

> not

> *Jenna had twins last year, her sister has twins too.* (comma splice)

> *Jenna had twins last year her sister has twins too.* (run-on sentence)

> *Many Mexicans leave Mexico* **because** *they cannot find jobs.* (complex sentence)

> not

> *Many Mexicans leave Mexico, they cannot find jobs.* (comma splice)

> *Many Mexican leave Mexico they cannot find jobs.* (run-on sentence)

6. Transitions can also be used to show the relationship between two sentences. Transitions show time, order, examples, additional and contrasting ideas, results, and conclusions. See the following chart for some common transitions.

The tour stopped at the Statue of Liberty. **Next,** *it went to the Empire State Building.*

Students write many different types of paragraphs. **For example,** *there are compare and contrast, cause and effect, narrative, and descriptive paragraphs.*

All the applicants are outstanding. **However,** *only one can get the job.*

A comma will generally follow a transition. Writers can use a semicolon instead of a period before transitions.

Colin had a math exam; then, he had to review for his history final.

TIME	EXAMPLE	ADDITION	CONTRAST	RESULT	CONCLUSION
first/second/etc.	for example	also	however	therefore	in conclusion
first of all	for instance	in addition	in contrast	consequently	to conclude
next	as a first/second/final example	moreover	on the other hand	as a result	
then		furthermore			
after that					
finally					
meanwhile					

7. A run-on sentence or a comma splice happens when two independent clauses are combined without a period, conjunction, or transition. There are four ways to fix a run-on sentence or a comma splice.

- Make two separate sentences by using a period or a semicolon. A semicolon signals that the two sentences are closely related. It is similar to the conjunction *and*.

  Hoa and Jeffery are the valedictorians they have 4.5 GPAs (run-on sentence)

  Hoa and Jeffery are valedictorians. They have 4.5 GPAs.

  Hoa and Jeffery are valedictorians; they have 4.5 GPAs.

- Make two separate sentences by using a transition that shows the relationship between the two sentences. Use either a period or a semicolon to separate the two sentences and a comma after the transition.

  We loved the book, the movie was terrible (comma splice)

  We loved the book. However, the movie was terrible.

  We loved the book; however, the movie was terrible.

- Use a coordinating conjunction to combine two independent clauses and show their relationship to each other.

  We missed the lecture, we need to borrow your notes. (comma splice)

  We missed the lecture, so we need to borrow your notes.

- Use a subordinating conjunction to combine two independent clauses and show their relationship to each other.

    They moved to Arizona the weather is warm there. (run-on sentence)

    They moved to Arizona because the weather is warm there.

    Because the weather is warm in Arizona, they moved there.

<table>
<tr><td>WRITING TIP</td></tr>
<tr><td>Semicolons are a good way to show a close relationship between two sentences. However, do not use them too often. Notice how little you see semicolons in the reading that you do.</td></tr>
</table>

8. A sentence that is missing a subject or a verb is called a fragment.

    Takes the subway to work every day. (fragment — missing subject)

    My friend takes the subway to work every day.

    The subway very crowded at rush hour. (fragment — missing verb)

    The subway is very crowded at rush hour.

    They getting off at the next stop. (fragment — missing auxiliary or helping verb)

    They are getting off at the next stop.

    Because the bus is slow. (fragment — missing independent clause)

    Because the bus is slow, people prefer the subway.

9. A phrase is not a complete sentence because it does not have a subject and a verb. A phrase by itself is a fragment. Therefore, a phrase is always combined with an independent clause. One of the most common types of phrases is a prepositional phrase. A prepositional phrase includes a preposition and a noun.

    in the Humanities Lecture Hall (prepositional phrase)

    In the Humanities Lecture Hall, the class is taking an exam. (prepositional phrase + independent clause)

    The class is taking an exam in the Humanities Lecture Hall. (independent clause + prepositional phrase)

    next to my computer (prepositional phrase)

    Next to my computer, there is a pile of books. (prepositional phrase + independent clause)

    There is a pile of books next to my computer. (independent clause + prepositional phrase)

Self Check

Circle the sentence with the correct sentence structure.

1. **a.** Every Friday in the restaurant on the corner.

   b. We eat dinner every Friday in the restaurant on the corner.

2. **a.** My aunt and uncle are living in Chile.

   b. My aunt and uncle living in Chile.

3. **a.** Because they love scuba diving, they went to Cozumel for their honeymoon.

   b. They love scuba diving, they went to Cozumel for their honeymoon.

4. **a.** Lupita has a nice personality so she has a lot of friends.

   b. Lupita has a nice personality, so she has a lot of friends.

5. **a.** The weather is beautiful today we're going to the beach.

   b. The weather is beautiful today; we're going to the beach.

WRITING TIP

Good writers use a variety of sentence types and lengths in their writing. They use both short and long sentences as well as simple, compound, and complex sentences. Always look at your sentence types and lengths when you are editing. Your writing will be more interesting and fun to read if it has a variety of sentence types.

EDITING PRACTICE

1. *Put a check (✓) next to the sentences that use sentence structure and punctuation correctly. Correct the sentences that have errors.*

_____ **1.** Australia is a continent; it is also an island.

_____ **2.** Jeannie still lives with her parents. Consequently, she has saved a lot of money.

_____ **3.** Unemployment is bad, people lose their salary and their benefits.

_____ **4.** Because there was a lot of rain last winter, the city is allowing people to water their yards this summer.

_____ **5.** Mr. Holmes driving home right now.

_____ **6.** In the kitchen on the shelf above the sink.

_____ **7.** Computer stores sell many products. For example, computers, printers, and software.

_____ **8.** In Japan, Golden Week includes four holidays over seven days.

_____ **9.** Since Abul arrived in the U.S., he has taken three English classes.

_____ **10.** We wanted organic vegetables but the store didn't have any.

_____ **11.** Her uncle died.

2. *Choose the correct punctuation from the choices given. Ø means that no punctuation is needed.*

How do we describe each generation of children_____ First, each
<u>1.? / !</u>

generation has a special name that distinguishes it from other generations.

For example_____ the Silent Generation includes people born between
<u>2.. / ,</u>

1925 and 1945. These children were born between the two world wars_____
<u>3.. / ,</u>

but they were not old enough to fight in World War II. The Baby Boom

Generation came between 1946 and 1964_____ A large increase in the birth
<u>4., / .</u>

rate is the most important characteristic of this generation. Baby Boomers

also include the hippies from the 1960s. When the Baby Boomers became

adults and had children _____ their children were called Generation X. This
<u>5., / .</u>

generation grew up in the 1980s and 1990s. Between the 1980s and early

2000s_____ Generation Y was born. In addition to the name Generation Y_____
<u>6.. / ,</u>   <u>7., / .</u>

this generation is also called the Millennial Generation or Millennials. The

children of this generation grew up with technology_____ such as the
<u>8.. / Ø</u>

personal computer, the mobile phone, and other portable devices. The most

recent generation is Generation Z. What events or inventions will describe

this generation_____ Only the future can answer this question. However_____
<u>9.. / ?</u>   <u>10., / ;</u>

history has shown us that this generation will have characteristics that are

very different from the earlier generations.

3. *The underlined parts of this paragraph contain errors with run-on sentences, fragments, or comma splices. Make the necessary corrections to correct the sentence structure.*

Is a formal education necessary for success? Most people believe that we need at least a high school diploma for a successful life. <u>However, there are millionaire and billionaire dropouts these people show us that not everyone needs a degree to succeed.</u> <u>For example, Jay-Z is a multimillionaire rapper, he doesn't have a high school diploma but he controls his million-dollar records, tours, and endorsements.</u> Carl Linder is worth $1.7 billion. <u>After Linder dropped out of high school to deliver milk for his family's dairy.</u> He opened an ice cream shop and ran different businesses to create his huge wealth. <u>Another millionaire dropout he is George Foreman.</u> <u>Foreman was a champion boxer, now he is a successful businessman and sells many different products.</u> <u>From the television show *American Idol* and his other businesses.</u> Simon Cowell earned $75 million last year. <u>Cowell dropped out of school at fifteen however he still became successful.</u> <u>When Richard Branson dropped out of school at fifteen.</u> He started a magazine. Since that time, he has built the Virgin Group. <u>This group includes 200 companies in thirty different countries Branson is worth $3.2 billion.</u> Even though most people agree that an education helps us succeed, these examples prove that not everyone needs a diploma.

4. *The following paragraph has no punctuation. Add the correct punctuation and capitalization.*

When people buy a new car, they have to make many decisions. First of all, the price of a car is important. An economy car has a low price, but it may have high fuel costs. On the other hand, an alternative-fuel car may cost more but have better fuel economy. As a result, alternative fuel cars may be more economical when someone keeps the car for a long time. In addition to price, a car's environmental impact is important. Many gasoline-powered cars are becoming more fuel efficient, yet they still pollute the environment. In contrast, some alternative-fuel vehicles produce no pollutants. Besides the cost and environmental impact, the resale value of a car is important. Small economy cars keep some of their value, but alternative-fuel cars keep almost all of their value. Consequently, an alternative fuel car will cost less over the years and help the environment more than traditional gas-powered vehicles.

WRITING TOPICS

Read the student's paragraph about the writing process. Notice the sentence variety used. The paragraph includes a clear topic sentence, supporting sentences, and a concluding sentence. Use this as a model when you write a paragraph about one of the topics below.

When my teacher gives me a writing assignment, I always follow the same process. First, I read the topic carefully and brainstorm by myself. I write all of my ideas on a piece of paper. Before I begin to write the formal paragraph, I always discuss my ideas with my friends, family, and tutors in the Writing Center. This step helps me choose my best ideas and focus my draft. Next, I sit down in front of my computer and write. After I finish writing, I save my paragraph and don't look at it for a day. In twenty-four hours, I read my paragraph again. Sometimes, I add new information, take out unnecessary details, and move sentences to new locations. After that, I work on editing for grammar, mechanics, and vocabulary errors. However, I don't do this immediately. I can edit better when I wait a few hours or days. Finally, the paragraph is ready to turn in. This is the writing process that my teachers recommend, and it works very well for me.

Choose one of the topics and write one paragraph. Use a variety of sentence types and lengths in your paragraph. After you complete your first draft, concentrate on editing your work. Keep in mind the editing practice from this chapter.

1. Tell the story about how you met someone important in your life. For example, tell how you met your husband, wife, best friend, long-lost cousin, or neighbor.

2. Describe your writing process. Explain how you write a paragraph, an essay, or a letter from the beginning to the end.

Go to page 124 for more practice with sentence structure and punctuation.

Commonly Confused Words

GRAMMAR FOCUS

Accurate and natural writing depends on vocabulary as much as grammar. By studying and practicing commonly confused words, you can avoid some common errors that writers make with these words. Notice how the two sentences below are the same except for one word, yet one sentence is considered correct and the other incorrect.

| We **made** our homework last night. (incorrect) | We **did** our homework last night. (correct) |

Pretest

Check your understanding of commonly confused words. Put a check (✓) next to the sentences that are correct.

_____ **1.** The referee told the soccer player to leave the game.

_____ **2.** We looked at an exciting movie last night.

_____ **3.** They are used to living on campus now, but it was difficult at first.

_____ **4.** Roger was required to write about his believes in philosophy.

_____ **5.** The company emphasis continuing education for employees.

_____ **6.** If you don't get enough sleep it will effect your work.

_____ **7.** There blog is about the next presidential election.

_____ **8.** The Pacific Ocean is larger than the Atlantic Ocean.

_____ **9.** Airlines loose people's luggage every day.

_____ **10.** Students have to make their homework daily.

GRAMMAR IN CONTEXT

Some of the commonly confused words that are presented in this chapter are underlined in the paragraph below. Notice the underlined words and think about why the writer may have chosen to use them.

Many people <u>believe</u> that Valentine's Day is the most important celebration of the year because <u>it's</u> the day that celebrates love. Valentine's Day <u>used to</u> have no connection to romance, but in modern times, it has become a popular day to show love and friendship. <u>There</u> are many ways that people express <u>their</u> love. For example, in the United States, men may <u>bring</u> flowers to women, while in Japan women <u>bring</u> chocolate to their love interests, friends, and colleagues. Other countries celebrate romance <u>too</u>, but not on Valentine's Day. In China they celebrate the Night of the Sevens, and in Iran they have Sepandarmazgan. <u>They're</u> similar to Valentine's Day but have a completely different history. While the history and dates are different, there are more similarities <u>than</u> differences in celebrations of love and friendship throughout the world.

Verbs

Be

Be is followed by adjectives.

> The beach **is** beautiful today.

> The book **is** interesting.

The verb *be* can be followed by a noun if the subject and the noun are the same person or thing.

> My brother **is** a lawyer.

> Camille's cousin **is** a wonderful artist.

Have

Have is followed by nouns.

> I **have** the flu.

> She **has had** the same job for six years.

Make

Make usually shows that something new is created.

> We **made** a delicious dinner.

> Andre is **making** many new friendships at work.

Use *make* in the following common expressions: *make a difference, make a mess, make a mistake, make money, make progress, make trouble.*

Do

Do usually refers to work or activities that someone must complete.

> The class **does** vocabulary exercises every day.

> Jamal **did** the shopping for our party.

Use *do* in the following common expressions: *do the cooking, do the housework, do the laundry, do homework, do nothing, do someone a favor, do your best.*

Know

Know shows that someone is familiar or acquainted with another person, place, or thing.

> *I* **have known** *him since last year.*

> *He* **knows** *London well because he lived there last year.*

Meet

Meet refers to the first time someone is introduced to another person.

> *We* **met** *each other last year.*

> *My fiancé* **will meet** *my parents next weekend.*

Say

Say is used when we do not know who the listener is. It is used without the object.

> *The school counselor* **said** *that we should finish our math requirement soon.*

> *The newspaper* **says** *that the weather will be sunny this week.*

Tell

Tell is used when we know who the listener is. It is used with the object.

> *The doctor* **tells** *her patients to exercise regularly.*

> *The policeman* **told** *the driver the directions to the police station.*

Note that in the following common expressions the listener is not always mentioned: *tell the truth, tell a lie, tell a story, tell a joke, tell a secret, tell the time.*

See

See is used when we notice something unexpectedly that we were not looking for. This is also what we do without thinking about it (a blind person cannot see).

> *I* **saw** *Lucia at the gym yesterday.*

> *Did you* **see** *that accident on the freeway?*

Look

Look is a voluntary action when we use our eyes to focus on an object. It is usually for a short period of time.

> *We* **looked** *at the menu but didn't like the choices.*

> *I always* **look** *at my answers before turning in my exams.*

Watch

Watch is used when we look at something for a period of time. It is usually moving.

> *We* **watched** *a movie last night.*

> *It's important to* **watch** *your children when they are in the pool.*

Take

Take is used when we carry something to the place that we are going or away from where the speaker is.

> *I am* **taking** *dessert to the party tonight.*

> *Have you* **taken** *your car to the mechanic?*

Bring

Bring means to carry something to the place where the speaker is.

> *Can you **bring** a salad to my party this weekend?*

> *The professor told the students they could **bring** their laptops to class.*

Used to

Used to refers to something that happened regularly in the past but doesn't happen anymore.

> *They **used to** eat meat, but now they are vegetarians.*

> *Mr. Ham **used to** play computer games until the games became violent.*

Be used to + –ing

Be used to + –ing refers to something that is normal or not unusual.

> *Farmers are **used to getting** up before sunrise.*

> *Teachers are **used to having** long summer vacations.*

Get used to + –ing

Get used to + –ing refers to the process of becoming familiar or comfortable with something.

> *Alfredo **got used to speaking** English when he moved to the United States.*

> *It took me some time to **get used to doing** homework on the weekends.*

Self Check 1

Circle the letter of the sentence that uses words or phrases correctly.

1. **a.** We met the candidates at an event last night.

   b. We knew the candidates at an event last night.

2. **a.** The technician told the computer system was not working.

   b. The technician told us the computer system was not working.

3. **a.** The students watched their notes before the exam.

   b. The students looked at their notes before the exam.

4. **a.** We used to communicate by e-mail but now we text.

   b. We are used to communicate by e-mail but now we text.

5. **a.** Redwood trees can have over 2,000 years.

   b. Redwood trees can be over 2,000 years old.

Noun-Verb Pairs

The following pairs of nouns and verbs are commonly confused because of their similar spelling.

Advice (uncountable noun)

> *She gave me some good **advice**.*

Advise (verb)

> *I **advised** him not to drop the class.*

Effect (count noun)

> *Jim's problems had a negative **effect** on his work.*

Affect (verb)

> *Jim's problems **affected** his work.*

Belief (count noun)

> *They have strong **beliefs**.*

Believe (verb)

> *They **believe** in truth and justice.*

Breath (count noun)

> *She can see her **breath** in the cold air.*

Breathe (verb)

> *Babies **breathe** deeply while they are sleeping.*

Emphasis (uncountable noun)

> *The mayor's speech had an **emphasis** on public safety.*

Emphasize (verb)

> *The mayor's speech **emphasized** public safety.*

WRITING TIP

To improve your English vocabulary, use it! Make friends with English speakers, watch English television shows and movies, and read English magazines, newspapers, and books. Notice how the vocabulary is used in all of these settings.

Pronouns, Possessive Adjectives, and Contractions

Its

Its is a possessive adjective just like *his, her*, or *your*. It always comes before a noun.

> *The dog is happy. **Its** tail is wagging.*

It's

It's is a contraction of *it is* or *it has*.

> ***It's** a beautiful day today.*

> ***It's** been a long time since we saw each other.*

There

There is an adverb that means a specific location.

> *Pamela wants to go **there** for graduate school.*

There is a pronoun that shows something happens or exists.

> ***There** is a lot of information on the class website.*

Their

Their is a possessive adjective. It always comes before a noun.

> *The children spent the night at **their** house.*

They're

They're is the contraction of *they are*.

> ***They're** at school right now.*

Whose

Whose is a possessive adjective.

> **Whose** *books are on the floor?*

Who's

Who's is the contraction of *who is* or *who has*.

> **Who's** *on the phone?*

> **Who's** *lived in Texas before?*

Your

Your is a possessive adjective. It always comes before a noun.

> *Mrs. Kendall has* **your** *house key.*

You're

You're is the contraction of you are.

> **You're** *a good singer and actor.*

WRITING TIP

To help increase your vocabulary and use the words correctly, create a personal vocabulary list of words that you confuse often, or make flashcards of new words that you want to learn.

Other Easily Confused Words

Then

Then is a transition meaning at that time.

> *They went for a run.* **Then** *they went swimming.*

Than

Than is a conjunction with comparatives.

> *They do more running* **than** *swimming.*

> *Adin is taller* **than** *his older brother is now.*

To

To is a preposition when it comes before a noun.

> *We walked* **to** *the store.*

To is an infinitive when it comes before a verb.

> *He wants* **to** *see a movie tonight.*

Too

Too means *also*.

> *I'm taking drawing class, but I want to take a painting class* **too**.

Too also means *in excess* and comes before an adjective or adverb.

> *It is* **too** *smoggy today for the children to be outside.*

> *You are playing the music* **too** *loudly.*

Two

Two is a number.

> *Latika has* **two** *brothers.*

Lose

Lose is a verb that means something is misplaced or you are unable to find something. The past tense is *lost*.

> *He frequently* **loses** *his car keys.*

Loose

Loose is an adjective that means the opposite of *tight*.

> *She has been on a diet, and her pants are* **loose**.

Self Check 2

Circle the word that completes the sentence correctly.

1. They (advised / adviced) us to carry an emergency kit in our car.

2. Weather can (affect / effect) a person's mood.

3. People with asthma (breath / breathe) with difficulty.

4. They (belief / believe) cancer can be cured this decade.

5. The university supplies laptops for (its / it's) students.

6. We are going to (there / their) wedding next month.

7. The doctor (who's /whose) in the operating room is a surgeon.

8. (Your / You're) responsible for completing the work on time.

9. It is raining in Seattle and in Portland (too / to).

10. The boutique's prices are more expensive (than / then) the department store's prices.

11. It is stylish to wear (lose / loose) pants.

12. The Choi family is going to Vietnam. (Then / Than), they will travel to Laos and Cambodia.

> ### WRITING TIP
> See Appendix 4 for a list of adjective and preposition combinations and verb and preposition combinations. Like the list of words in this chapter, the words in Appendix 4 are easily confused.

EDITING PRACTICE

1. *Put a check (✓) next to the sentences that use the commonly confused words correctly. Correct the sentences that have errors.*

_____ **1.** Teenagers generally ask for advice from their friends.

_____ **2.** My speech teacher emphasis the importance of clear pronunciation.

_____ **3.** Good swimmers do not breathe on every stroke.

_____ **4.** The tallest buildings in the world have over 2,000 feet.

_____ **5.** The snow effected the wild flowers last spring.

_____ **6.** Whose going to the retirement luncheon?

_____ **7.** The river looks clean, but your not supposed to drink the water.

_____ **8.** Did you know Blanca at the meeting last week?

_____ **9.** The bank may loose customers if it changes locations.

_____ **10.** Please take a salad to my house tonight.

_____ **11.** Ariel's music is too loud.

_____ **12.** Did you watch the Picasso painting in the museum?

2. *Complete the paragraph with the correct verb forms.*

Research has shown that birth order _____ a
                                          1. effect / affects

child's personality. This is definitely true in my family. The order that my

brother and sisters were born _____ me a lot about
                                    2. tells / says

_____ personalities. Supporting what some research
  3. there / their

_____, my oldest brother is smarter _____
  4. tells / says   **5. than / then**

my other siblings, and he makes more money _____.
                                                  6. too / to

Even when we were growing up, he _____ have the most
                                    7. used to / was used to

money in his bank account. My middle sisters are the ones who make sure

everyone gets along in the family. When _____ are
                                              8. there / their

disagreements, _____ the ones to stop them. I am the
                  9. they're / their

youngest and the most flexible in the family. I can _____
                                                        10. be used to / get used to

anything quickly because I have had to compromise my entire life. After

watching my brother and sisters for many years, I _____
                                                      11. believe / belief

that birth order has helped shape their personalities.

3. *In the following paragraph, the underlined words are not correct. Write the correct word above each underlined error.*

Every year millions of Americans get new cell phones. All of the old

phones, PDAs, chargers, and batteries used to take up a lot of space in

landfills. Now many people recycle <u>there</u> old electronic devices. <u>Their</u> are
                                1   2

several benefits to this. First of all, recycling saves energy. Cell phones and

PDAs are made of materials that take energy <u>too</u> manufacture. By recycling
                    3

these materials, they can be turned into other products. This also helps <u>too</u>
                    4

keep the toxic materials that <u>effect</u> human health out of the ground. Second,
          5

donated phones can be reused by people who need them. Finally, <u>its</u> possible
          6

to sell <u>you're</u> old cell phone. <u>Than</u>, the phone can be sold at a low cost to
       7   8

someone who can use it. After you buy a new cell phone or PDA, <u>see</u> for
          9

a company or organization that recycles them. It helps others and the

environment <u>to</u>.
      10

4. *The following paragraph has ten errors with the use of commonly confused words. Find and correct the errors.*

Once when I was in New York City, I knew a pickpocket. We were riding

on the same bus during rush hour, and I saw him bring wallets from the

pockets of two men. Than, he saw a woman who's purse was open. I was

about to tell something, but I was so nervous that I couldn't breath. At that

moment, red lights began flashing behind the bus, and the bus pulled over.

The pickpocket saw what was happening and quickly returned the two wallets

to the men's pockets. I couldn't belief my eyes; nobody looked at any of this.

A police officer stepped onto the bus and searched the pickpocket, but their

was no evidence in his pockets. Everyone on the bus told the police officer that they weren't missing anything. As the police officer stepped off the bus,

he adviced us to always keep our wallets in a safe place.

WRITING TOPICS

Read the student's paragraph about the qualities of the person who raised him or her. Circle some commonly confused words from this chapter. The paragraph includes a clear topic sentence, supporting sentences, and a concluding sentence. Use this paragraph as a model when you write a paragraph about one of the topics below.

Although nobody is perfect, my mother has many qualities that make a good parent. She was only nineteen when I was born, but she already knew how to raise a child. First of all, she gave me a lot of freedom. I used to explore my surroundings from morning to night. She wanted to know what I was doing and where I was, but she trusted me. She still gives me the freedom to study the major I want and to choose the career that is best for me. My mother also gives me good advice but not too much of it. She always tells me her opinion, but she doesn't continue to emphasize it. While I was growing up, she used to encourage me to get advice from many different people and then make the best decision from all of those opinions. I still do this today when I have a big decision to make. Another good quality my mother has is optimism. She has always told me to look at the positive side of any difficult situation. This was especially helpful when we moved to the United States when I was ten years old. Her positive attitude helped me meet many new friends and adapt to the new environment very quickly. I believe that my mother's many good qualities have helped make me the successful person that I am today.

Choose one of the topics and write one paragraph. Use as many words as possible from the list of commonly confused words in this chapter. After you complete your first draft, concentrate on editing your work. Keep in mind the editing practice from this chapter.

1. Write about one of your parents or the person who raised you. Discuss the good or bad qualities that this person has and how the qualities influenced your life. Give specific examples that show these qualities.

2. How does money affect the way that people behave? Write about the positive or negative influence that money has on people who have money or on people that do not have money.

Go to page 126 for more practice with commonly confused words.

Extra Editing Practice

Use the following pieces of writing to practice editing for grammar points that you have focused on in the previous chapters.

When you edit your own writing, it is important to look for many different grammatical errors; therefore, the exercises in this chapter require that you edit for more than one type of grammatical structure at a time.

> **WRITING TIP**
>
> When you edit your essay for grammar, you will need to read the essay many times. You will find your grammar errors more easily if you check for only one grammatical point at a time.

Present Time and Subject-Verb Agreement

1. *Edit carefully for verb errors in the present and in subject-verb agreement. There are ten errors in the following paragraph.*

After most students graduate from college, they have found jobs and begin earning money. Recently, nontraditional jobs have become popular. Today graduates are exploring careers in nonprofit, public service, and government organizations that were not popular in the past. Over the past decade, students has chosen from many types of employers and selected the jobs that is the best for them. Sometimes nontraditional jobs may not pay the most money; however, the knowledge that new graduates gain in low-paying positions are very valuable. Spending two or three years in the Peace Corps or Teach America help new workers learn about themselves and the world. The sacrifice in pay that a recent graduate make will hopefully be made up for in future positions. In addition to future job benefits, a person gains friends and experiences that are worth more than money. In other words, the sacrifices that graduates makes early in their careers will be rewarded sooner or later. New opportunities are coming from unexpected places, and students are knowing that many times nontraditional work is that unexpected place. These kinds of opportunities are available throughout life, but the time to begin looking for them are now.

Past Time and Subject-Verb Agreement

2. *Edit carefully for verb errors in the past and in subject-verb agreement. There are ten errors in the following essay.*

I had always wanted to learn more about rain forests, and my opportunity was arriving last spring. My university organized a group of biology students to work and study in Central America. I had signed up right away.

The location where we lived and studied were one of the best places in Central America to observe the rain forest. In my first few moments there, I saw many plants and animals that the rain forest was containing. During the two months I was being there, I saw plants and animals that I never known before. The rain forest's diversity were incredible to all the students in my group. We even had the opportunity to discover a plant that scientists have never seen before. Studying in this environment with so many plants and animals was the best experience of my life.

When I was returning from the rain forest, I committed myself to improving our environment. I had recommended this kind of work and study program to all my fellow students. People from all fields should have this type of experience to appreciate the world that we live in.

Time Shifts and Future Time

3. *Edit carefully for errors in time shifts and future time. There are ten errors in the following paragraph.*

Why didn't I stop the thieves? Why didn't I call the police? Why didn't I do anything to help? In horror, I stood up from my hiding place in the convenience store as the thieves were running out of the door. At that moment, I felt fear that I never knew before. Since then, I am experiencing a lot of guilt for not helping during that robbery. Even though I have a cell phone at the time, I did not think about calling the police. In general, I know that fear caused people to behave in unexpected ways. However, until that moment, I believe I was a fearless person. At that instant, I saw a side of myself that I am still not proud of. I hoped that in the future, I will behave differently. I try to be braver. I now know that the shame I feel today is worse than the fear I feel on that day. Those few seconds teach me the importance of doing the right thing. This is a lesson that I think changes my future behavior.

Count and Uncountable Nouns; Articles and Other Determiners

4. *Edit carefully for errors in count and uncountable nouns as well as in articles and other determiners. There are ten errors in the following paragraph.*

It was a cold night in the middle of winter, but the bright yellow stars made the 35-degrees night seem warmer. It wasn't cold enough to snow although there was some snows on the ground. I was driving my car past much houses along the road. I imagined the people behind each front doors enjoying family gathering and a nice dinner. All I felt was sadnesses and loneliness. My usual positive outlook was gone. I shook my head and tried to stop the sad thoughts. Thinking too much wasn't going to help situation. I tried to concentrate only on driving along the empty road. The significances of a moment was not clear to me at the time. It would become obvious in the next few hour.

Pronouns; Demonstrative and Possessive Adjectives

5. *Edit carefully for errors in pronouns and demonstrative and possessive adjectives. There are ten errors in the following paragraph.*

I learned an important lesson about friendship when I was fourteen years old. Me and my family were living in a small town. The town didn't have many after-school activities other than playing basketball and hanging out. I thought I was good at both activities and did it whenever I could. Even though I played with him almost every day, the good players didn't think I played well enough to join his competitive team. After I noticed that all the competitive players wore NBA basketball jerseys, I convinced my parents to buy me two team jerseys. I was certain that I would be invited to play if I wore this jerseys. It was a very sad day for myself when I still wasn't asked to join the team. Not long afterwards, my family moved, and I made new friends in ours new town, but I'll never forget the lesson that I learned about competition and friendship. Friendship may be strong between my friends and I, but winning always comes first. Life lessons are sometimes hard to learn, but if a child does not learn it, they will have a hard time surviving in the real world.

Sentence Structure and Commonly Confused Words

6. *Edit carefully for errors in sentence structure and commonly confused words. There are ten errors in the following paragraph.*

When we use e-mail, its important to follow some rules these rules are called netiquette. Netiquette is similar to regular etiquette but with an emphasize on online communication. The first netiquette rule is to never argue by e-mail. When something maddening happens. It is better to meet in person and talk over the problem. Another important rule of netiquette is to edit e-mail messages carefully. Nobody likes to watch a message full of grammar errors and misspelled words. Finally, writing a message in all capital letters is like yelling at someone therefore always follow normal capitalization rules in e-mail. Even though most people use e-mail frequently many companies belief netiquette is very important, and they send there employees to classes on it. They're also many books on the topic of netiquette. It's crucial to show respect online. Because online communication is just as important as face to face communication is.

Modals and Verb Tense

7. *Edit carefully for errors in modals and verb tense. There are ten errors in the following paragraph.*

Service animals can often help people with disabilities. For nearly 100 years, disabled people use these animals to improve their lives. Blind World War I veterans use guide dogs in the 1920s. Since that time, guide dogs help blind people cross the street, avoid obstacles, and locate objects. Large, strong dogs should do these kinds of jobs. This is why people are now training miniature horses for many of the same tasks. Hearing-impaired or deaf

105

people might also to use a service dog that can alert them when a doorbell rings, a baby cries, a smoke alarm goes off, or a telephone rings. Like dogs and miniature horses, monkeys are sometimes service animals. People first train monkey helpers during the 1970s. Quadriplegics, people without use of their arms and legs, have to use monkey helpers to get a glass of water, pick up items on the floor, and turn lights on and off. Some service animals can help people who have seizures. The animal must notices small changes in the person before a seizure. By licking or whining, the animal would warn the person to get into a safe position. Finally, ill or elderly people are supposed to benefit from the emotional support of an animal. These therapy animals may being dogs, cats, or sometimes horses. Animals have certainly improved the lives of many people with disabilities.

APPENDIX 1: PRACTICE WITH AUTHENTIC LANGUAGE

Chapter 1: Expressing Present Time

*Read the following selection from the **Newport Beach Light** newspaper. Choose the correct form of the verb.*

many talents

Triple Threat

by Scott Barajas

Jillianne Whitfield _____**loves**_____ to play basketball,
1. loves / is loving

[play] soccer, and run track. But her real passion is on the diamond,[1] playing

footnote

baseball with the boys.

"There's no action in girls' softball. It's too slow for me," said Jillianne.
"I ___**have played**___ *present perfect* baseball since I was in first grade." When
2. have played / play

the 12-year-old multitalented athlete isn't kicking soccer balls and dribbling

basketballs, she ___**is swinging**___ the aluminum bat and
3. is swinging / has swung

chattering with teammates.

"I got started playing hardball because I wanted to give it a try," said

Jillianne. "I loved playing my first year, and I ___**haven't stopped**___
4. am not stopping / haven't stopped

playing since."

While Jillianne waits for the baseball season to start, she keeps busy playing

basketball for the Costa Mesa Warriors and playing soccer for Newport Mesa.

Every Sunday, the 5-foot 6-inch Whitfield ___**displays**___
5. displays / is displaying

her basketball skills at various gyms around the county. Head Coach George Grant

says Jillianne is a creator on the court. Creating shots and making crisp passes are

reasons her teammates compare her to Michael Jordan.

[1] **diamond** baseball playing field

OC Register. Reprinted with permission.

"Jillianne _____**is**_____ [handwritten: *adverb (describes the verb) -ly*] consistently around the ball

6. is being / is

and she plays good defense," he said. "But her most valued basketball skill is her

ability to drive the lane and make off-balance lay-ups[2] on both sides of the basket,

which is why her teammates gave her the name of Ms. Jordan."

Jillianne laughs at the name, but she likes it.

"I guess my lay-ups resemble Michael Jordan's," said Jillianne, who right

now _____**is averaging**_____ 10 points and seven rebounds[3] a game.

7. has averaged / is averaging

Today, basketball _____**isn't taking up**_____ Jillianne's time, so she's

8. hasn't taken up / isn't taking up

off to the soccer fields, a sport she got into by mistake.

"My younger sister signed up and then didn't want to play, so I took her

place," she said. "But on the soccer field, I'm not the star. I'm average."

On the baseball diamond, Jillianne is one of the stars. The All-Star team

_____**has picked**_____ Jillianne for the last three years.

9. picks / has picked

"I _____**like**_____ to play defense. I consider myself a

10. like / am liking

better fielder[4] than a batter,"[5] said Jillianne, who plays first and third base.

Jillianne wants to continue to play baseball in high school in a couple of

years.

"I'm going to try out for boys' baseball, but if I don't make it, I'll switch to

basketball."

....

[2] **lay-ups** basketball shots near the basket

[3] **rebounds** catching the basketball after a missed shot

[4] **fielder** baseball player in the field; not at bat

[5] **batter** baseball player at bat

[handwritten: like | to play |
want | to go |
need | to finish |
infinitive]

Chapter 2: Expressing Past Time

*Read the following selection from the **Los Angeles Times**. Choose the correct form of the verb.*

Students Set Up Outdoor Library
by Carla Rivera

California State University, Los Angeles students Stephanie Velasquez and

Karla Chitay were stymied[1] recently when they headed to the university library to

study for final exams: The facility _____ at 8 p.m. just
1. had close / had closed

before they arrived.

But a few feet away, students were bent over laptops and textbooks in a

makeshift[2] open air study area. There was a copy machine and a printer. Coffee,

free of charge, _____ as a late evening chill began to
2. was brewing / had brewed

descend.

"We came to the library straight from class and when we found it closed, we

were like 'oh no, what are we going to do,'" said Valesquez, who like Chitay, is a

social work major. "We _____ to study together but we
3. were wanting / wanted

live on opposite sides of town . . ."

Since it _____ June 1, the so-called "People's
4. was opening / opened

Library" has been available until midnight each day. It was organized by a group

of students after administrators curtailed[3] regular library hours this year because of

state budget cuts.

....

[1] **stymied** prevented from doing something

[2] **makeshift** temporary

[3] **curtailed** restricted

Organizers contend that reduced access to library resources

_____ students' studies, especially in the weeks before
5. was affecting / were affecting

final exams. So they _____ donated chairs and tables
6. gathered / gather

and have been using campus electrical hookups for lighting and equipment just

outside the university's library. . . .

Organizers said Cal State administrators at first threatened to close down the

alternative operation and briefly turned off its electricity. . . .

They [facility officials] _____ students address
7. helped / had helped

safety issues such as securing electrical cords and there have been no incidents.

The library will hold its last session Thursday as finals week ends. The

Los Angeles campus, one of 23 in the Cal State system, is not alone in making

reductions in the face of a severe financial crisis. The library budget was cut 20%

this year . . . university librarian Alice Kawakami said.

The library also _____ full-time student
8. cut / cutted

assistant positions from 19 to 11 and _____
9. cancel / canceled

subscriptions to more than 400 print journals and 10 databases. The decision to

close the library at 8 p.m. rather than 10 p.m. _____
10. had come / came

after it was found that fewer students used it after 7 p.m. . . .

For now, organizers say the library is needed because some students don't

have Internet access at home or a quiet place to study.

Chapter 3: Subject-Verb Agreement

Read the following selection from **Coast** *magazine. Choose the correct form of the verb.*

A Very Able Crew

by Torence Loose

A sailboat may seem the most unfriendly of environments for a

wheelchair, but don't tell that to Captain Duncan Milne. For twenty years—since

he rode a motorcycle off a cliff in a desert race and lost the use of his legs—

he _____ proven critics wrong from his 62-foot

          1. has / have

traditional ketch.[1] Since 1990 he has put that spirit to good use, running Access

to Sailing, a program that _____ over 500 children

              2. introduce / introduces

and adults with disabilities to sailing each year. Milne is inspiring a crew of five

developmentally disabled overachievers to compete in this year's Newport to

Ensenada Race. For the second year, Milne will lead Team Independence in the

400-boat yacht regatta.[2]

Though Milne's shipmates are challenged with autism, Down

syndrome, and slight mental retardation,[3] they will not make any excuses

if they _____ finish well. "We're competing

        3. don't / doesn't

to win, no doubt about it," says Milne. Which is why he and his crew

_____ trained for the race for months and recently

       4. have / has

circumnavigated[4] Catalina Island from Dana Point, traveling 102 miles, much of it

in bad weather conditions. "I was really proud of the crew," says Milne.

....

[1] **ketch** a type of sailing boat with two masts for the sails

[2] **yacht regatta** a sailboat race

[3] **retardation** slow mental development

[4] **circumnavigated** gone completely around

....

Tracy Young, manager of community relations for Project

Independence, which aids those with developmental disabilities,

_____ the crew members couldn't be more thrilled.
        5. say /says

"They know that yachting is a pretty exclusive sport, so to be a part of the

preparation and race is a chance of a lifetime." And they earned it. Two of the crew

sailed in last year's race, and all had to try out for this year's team by undergoing

physical fitness and memory tests. Out of over 30 applicants, five made the team.

    Though their training _____ mostly been
                6. has / have

on Milne's ketch, Team Independence will sail a $1.5 million 43-foot trimaran.[5]

Training for the race _____ as much as $10,000 says
          7. costs / cost

Young; donations _____ it possible. Milne says they
        8. makes / make

_____ backing a winner, regardless of the results.
      9. is / are

    "Sometimes it can get a little frustrating out there," he says. "But then I

consider what an incredible effort they have all made and how far they have come.

Suddenly little errors in steering _____ a big deal—so
             10. isn't / aren't

we come in third instead of first."

....
[5] **trimaran** a boat with three hulls/floats

Chapter 4: Expressing Future Time

*Read the following selection from **New University**, the student newspaper from the University of California, Irvine. Choose the correct form of the verb.*

Arts in the "Real World"

by Tina Sustarsic and Michaela Baltasar

Most students look forward to their post-college lives with a mixture of excitement and trepidation.[1] For majors in the arts, going out into the "real world" means competing with other dancers, actors, musicians, and artists with years more experience. The excitement of doing what you love for a living is tempered[2] with the realization that the artist's life is often very difficult.

New University interviewed several graduating seniors from the School of the Arts on their hopes and worries for the future and their experiences at the university.

New University: What are your plans after graduation?

Sarah Reece (Dance): After I graduate, I _____
                                              1. get / will get
certified in Pilates.[3] I'm going to train other people and support

myself while I _____ in New York. I
                    2. audition / will audition
_____ to New York to audition for modern companies
       3. am moving / move
and teach as soon as my certification is completed.

Andrew Henkes (Drama): I _____ begin
                                      4. am going / am going to
by applying for positions as assistant directors or really any positions in theater

....

[1] **trepidation** fear, dread

[2] **tempered** softened or moderated

[3] **Pilates** an exercise program

....
New University Newspaper 5/29/2000. Reprinted with permission.

companies. I'm going to try to find a theater company or two or three that

I like and I _____ them and let them know that
6. **5. contact / am going to contact**

I'm interested in working. Even if I get stuck[4] waiting tables or something, I

_____ some theater work on my own.
6. am going to do / am doing

Lara Wallis (Music): I'm going to pursue graduate studies at the

Manhattan School of Music in New York City. I _____
7. am going to study / study

oboe with the principal oboist of the New York Philharmonic when I get to New

York.

New University: How well do you think your arts education has prepared

you to go out into the real world?

Henkes: I feel like I've learned a lot. It's hard to say, though. I really

_____ until I get out there.
8. am not knowing / won't know

Wallis: I think it's prepared me in terms of independence, like establishing

a home away from the place I originally grew up. I think it has prepared me

to go to the East Coast and live away from friends and family. The program in

Manhattan _____ many challenges, but I feel like I
9. will provide / will provides

have been ready to make that step forward.

New University: Do you have any worries or concerns about your plans?

Reece: Like any job, there is a lot of competition and I think it

_____ be a struggle, but I'm looking forward to it.
10. will / going to

....
[4] **get stuck** become unable to get away from a boring or unpleasant situation

Chapter 5: Time Shifts and Tenses

*Read the following selection from **The Independent**, a community newspaper from Southern California. Choose the correct verb tense.*

Stand-Up Sport

by Brian Lichterman

In the last few years, a new sport _____

1. takes / has taken

Southern California by storm.[1] Paddleboarding has become one of the fastest

growing sports across the country and _____ to places

2. is spreading / spreads

around the world.

The origins are somewhat murky.[2] Some believe the sport has Polynesian

and Hawaiian roots, as fishermen _____ stand up on

3. use to / used to

long canoe-like boards to get a better view when fishing.

The overall history is still a bit of a mystery, but the origins of Hoviesup, the

only local paddleboard manufacturer, is no mystery at all. Professional surfer Brian

Hovnanian, who _____ most of his life in Southern

4. spends / has spent

California, _____ Hoviesup five years ago and has

5. started / has started

never looked back.

"I _____ a pro surfer from 1975 to 1981,"

6. was / have been

Hovanian said. "I got into paddleboarding after I saw Laird Hamilton paddling in

Malibu."

Hamilton _____ paddleboarding as a way to

7. was using / is using

train for surfing that day. As Hovnanian _____ 50, he

8. approaches / was approaching

....

[1] **to take something by storm** to become popular very quickly

[2] **murky** unclear

....

Lichterman, Brian. "Stand Up Sport," *The Independent*, June 11, 2010. Reprinted with the permission of Newport Beach Independent, published by Firebrand Media, LLC.

was also looking for a way to keep his body fit for surfing. Paddleboarding filled

that need.

Paddleboarding _____ a terrific core workout
               9. has been / is

and is also great for muscle soreness. Because of the benefits of paddleboarding,

Hovnanian is now more into the sport of paddling than surfing.

Hovnanian began making paddleboards a few years ago and since then

_____ seven models with another new model due out
    10. is developing / has developed

next August.

"Our new board will be made of plastic and

_____ a different shape than our current models.
      11. will have / is having

It will be a great model for paddling in the harbor and will hopefully replace

kayaks on many of the yachts in the harbor," Hovnanian said. The new model

_____ drink holders and fishing rod holders.
    12. has also had / will also have

Chapter 6: Count and Uncountable Nouns

*Read the following selection from the **EL Gazette**. Choose the correct noun form.*

Dog Masters ESL

A dog brought in to the Royal Society for the Prevention of Cruelty to

Animals (RSPCA) near Manchester, England has made good progress after receiving

English _____.

         1. lesson / lessons

Workers initially thought the dog, a male border collie named Cent,

was deaf because he didn't respond to commands. But tests showed his

_____ was good.

      2. hearing / hearings

Puzzled RSPCA workers consulted their records on Cent and found

that he had been owned by a Polish _____

                             3. family / families

who could no longer care for him. As Luke Johnson, one of the animal

care _____ recalled, "It was only a few

      4. assistant / assistants

_____ later when it dawned on us that he must be

      5. day / days

used to hearing commands in Polish."

An Internet search provided Cent's handlers with some Polish

commands, and they contacted the Polish family that brought him in for

_____ with _____.

      6. help / helps   **7. pronunciation / pronunciations**

Once Cent started responding to commands in Polish, the

_____ started teaching him to react to basic

      8. staff / staffs

commands in English using a "reward-based" program. Within four months,

Cent had become bilingual. Now he is ready to find a new home, ideally one with

_____ aged above 10 and in a location where he can

      9. children / childrens

get a lot of _____, said the RSPCA.

         10. exercise / exercises

EL Gazette, March 2010. Printed with permission.

Chapter 7: Articles and Other Determiners

*Read the following selection from the **Daily Pilot** newspaper. Choose the correct article, quantifier, or demonstrative adjective.*

A Good Impression

by Jennifer Garrison

Standing in front of Vincent van Gogh's famous painting "The Potato

Eaters," Janella Godoy considered _____ painting
1. the / a / Ø

thoughtfully before making a pronouncement: "The painting is so dark. It is meant

to convey sadness. And look at the brush strokes."

Not bad for a sixth-grader at the Los Angeles County Museum of Art

for _____ first time. And scattered throughout
2. the / a / Ø

the museum's galleries where the sold-out "Van Gogh's Van Goghs" show

is temporarily visiting from the Van Gogh Museum in Amsterdam were

_____ pint-sized[1] art critics.
3. many / much

They're _____ feet shorter and several hundred
4. a little / a few

dollars less-expensively appointed[2] than most of the other museum-goers. And

they haven't mastered the fine art of pretentiously propounding[3] over paintings—

one young man referred to "that beautiful painting, 'The Potato Heads,' or

whatever."

But the 85 students from Harbor View Elementary School who spent Friday

at _____ museum have an appreciation of why Van
5. the / a / Ø

Gogh was _____ great artist.
6. the / a / Ø

....

[1] **pint-sized** small, young

[2] **appointed** dressed

[3] **pretentiously propounding** discussing in an exaggerated and showy way

"His work is very interesting because of the way he uses colors and his brush strokes," said Camilla Mooshayedi. "And he experimented with _____ art. First he was

7. the / an / Ø

_____ impressionist[4] painter, and then he picked up

8. the / an / Ø

other things."

The sixth-graders at Harbor View are such art fans that they raised the money for buses and tickets to the museum by selling another one of their favorite things: candy. "I'm amazed and so proud of them," said teacher Sharon Harrington, who along with teacher Scottia Evans organized

_____ trip. "You never know how much they're

9. the / a / Ø

listening, because they're sixth-graders and they have to be so cool. But they really know a lot."

To prepare themselves to understand the paintings,

_____ students in _____

10. the / a / Ø   11. this / these

sixth-grade classes tried their hand at Van Gogh's style.

"_____ student painted 'Starry Night,'" one

12. Several / Every / Many

sixth-grader said.

A docent[5] came over to _____ students.

13. the / a / Ø

"Sorry. 'Starry Night' is in Minneapolis," he said. No matter, shrugged the students. They had their own copies at home, and four more rooms of Van Gogh at the museum.

....

[4] **impressionist** a style of painting that creates effects with color

[5] **docent** a person who leads tours through museums or galleries

Chapter 8: Pronouns

Read the following selection from **Orange County Woman** *magazine. Choose the correct pronoun, possessive adjective, or demonstrative adjective.*

Giving Back the Gift
by Carroll Lachnit

When Santa Ana policemen cleaned out a dangerous neighborhood five

years ago, _____*They*_____ knew their job wasn't quite done. Scared residents . . .
        1. they / it

needed reassurance[1] that the area was safe again. So the police department

asked Virginia Avila, a mother of seven who lived in the Flower Street Park

neighborhood, to help _____ reclaim[2] the formerly drug-filled park. With
                        2. it / them

Avila in charge of a new neighborhood association, the park has been transformed.

Like Avila, the women whose stories appear here have different histories

and life paths. But they share a deep sense of giving back to the community that

supported _____ with gifts of time, money, and personal examples.
          3. themselves / them

With these gifts in mind, these women look forward to focusing on Latino youth.

Sofia Negron: The work that Sofia Negron does as community outreach

director for MOMS (Maternal Outreach Management System) Resource Center

is worlds away from her previous profession: assistant designer at Ocean Pacific

sportswear. Now _____ can be found recruiting both care providers and
                  4. she / it

clients for MOMS, a Santa Ana based nonprofit organization that offers medical

care, education, and support countywide to indigent[3] women who are pregnant or

have just had their babies.

....
[1] **reassurance** restored confidence

[2] **reclaim** to make something usable again

[3] **indigent** very poor

"_____ totally changed my life," she says of her career change six

5. They / It

years ago.

Sandy Garcia: The title of Sandy Garcia's first CD translates as *Stop*

Thinking. But _____ isn't advice she's taking. When Garcia, 18, isn't

6. that / those

singing at mariachi gigs or recording her new CD in Tijuana, _____

7. her / she

often can be found performing free for charity fund raisers or serving as a student

representative on the county's Human Relations Commission.

Teresa Saldivar: Teresa Saldivar sells jewelry, but that hardly tells her

whole story. She's a mainstay[4] in the Hispanic business community, co-chair for

the Orange County Hispanic Education Endowment Fund, and a role model for

both Latino and female business owners. Hispanic leaders she met in college

reinforced her faith in education.

"_____ inspired me to continue, and when I opened my own

8. They / He

business, I wanted to do the same thing for Hispanic youth. There's a need for

_____ to have a role model."

9. them / it

Maria Elena Avila: Maria Elena Avila is in the restaurant business—one

of the toughest, most time-consuming professions around. _____ family's

10. Her / Hers

seven-restaurant El Ranchito chain is a Southern California institution,[5] and Avila

owns both the Costa Mesa location and El Ranchito's high-end catering business.

Avila, 45, also is a founding member of the Orange County Hispanic

Education Endowment Fund, which recently passed its $1 million fundraising goal.

....

[4] **mainstay** main support or help

[5] **Southern California institution** well known in Southern California

*Read the following selection from the **Daily Bruin**, the school newspaper from the University of California, Los Angeles. Choose the correct modal and verb combination.*

This Time, the Interviewer Is in Spotlight
by Stephanie Sheh

It is intelligent and warm, understanding and sympathetic. Terry Gross's voice has been heard with some of the most famous people of our time, ranging from Wilt Chamberlain and Hillary Rodham Clinton to Tom Stoppard and Eric Clapton.

This Sunday, the host of National Public Radio's "Fresh Air" will be in Royce Hall to share a few interviews that went particularly well, but mostly those that were real catastrophes.[1]

Though known for her sincerity toward her guests, she is not afraid to ask tough questions and has had her share of walkouts.

It _____ be hard to imagine someone walking
    1. had better / may

out on an interviewer with such a friendly and calming voice, but Gross does not see it that way. Actually, the first time she heard her voice on the radio was during a recorded show. Aside from her roommates, Gross didn't tell anyone the program was airing. She felt the experience would be easier to survive if nobody listened.

"My brother called in the middle of the first program, and I told him that I was in the middle of a very important conversation

and I just _____ talk," Gross says. "I
         2. can't / couldn't

_____ lie to him. I _____
    3. had to / must   **4. couldn't / shouldn't**

tell him that the program was on."

....
¹ catastrophes dramatic events or disasters

....

Gross says she used to listen to her programs during her 30-minute

commute home from work. However, she now lives only five minutes away. Gross

_____ to tapes of shows for a
    5. may still occasionally listens / may still occasionally listen

"best of" of anthology[2] program.

"But there are times when the last thing in the world I want to do is hear

an interview again," Gross says. "Sometimes I think the unhealthiest thing I

_____ do is to spend an hour listening to myself on
            6. ought to / can

air."

By now however, Gross has accepted her voice. She says that though it does

not mean she loves it, now she _____ listen to it.
                                        7. can / can't

After all, Gross began hosting "Fresh Air" in 1985, when it was a weekly half-hour

program.

In 1987, though, the show turned into a daily, hour-long program. This

means that Gross now _____ conduct two interviews
                            8. must / have to

a day, prepare for upcoming interviews, and perform other duties for the program,

for which she is also a co-executive producer.

Gross says she reads as much as she can about a guest to prepare

for an interview. She _____ the artists' various
                        9. must also rent / must also rented

movies or listen to their records several times. Gross does as much as she

_____ but says that she still doesn't have as much
            10. could / can

preparation time as she would like.
....
[2] **anthology** a collection of literary pieces or programs

123

*Read the following selection from the **Daily Pilot** newspaper. Choose the correct punctuation.*

Worth the Right Word

by Tom Ragen

Girl Scouts[1] do more than sell cookies these days.

Paige Garcia, now a senior a Corona del Mar High School, is a good

example.

In less than a year _____ she shot more than 300 photographs
1. , / .

of basic life necessities, sat down at her computer, and converted them into

an educational package for special needs[2] students in the Mission Viejo School

District.

When school districts were struggling with state cutbacks _____
2. , / .

Garcia managed to save the school district time and money while helping about 50

families whose special needs children have a hard time communicating.

For this project _____ Garcia was one of seven Girls Scouts in
3. Ø / ,

her Newport Harbor Troop to receive the Gold Award, one of Scouting's highest

honors. However _____ perhaps more importantly, she is a sign of the
4. , / Ø

times _____ She is a Girl Scout who managed to come up with a computer
5. , / .

program that will be put to practical use by a school district.

Bill Thompson, a school psychologist with the Orange County Department

of Education, was amazed by the lightening speed[3] that Garcia managed to help

---

1 Girl Scouts an organization of girls founded in 1912 to develop citizenship, health, and character

2 special needs mentally or physically disabled

3 lightening speed very fast

---

the district _____ while she was juggling[4] the normal tasks of a junior in
   6. Ø / ,

high school.

Thompson said he plans to hand the discs over to special needs families

who can use the photographs inside their homes _____ when their special
                                              7. , / Ø

needs children have a hard time coming up with a word.

Garcia is known as an "ambassador" within her troop _____
                                                    8. , / Ø

because she is a couple of years older than the age limit. She went out on her own

and took photographs of all sorts of stuff. Garcia spent hundreds of hours taking

photos, downloading, organizing, and labeling them.

In all, she spent about $200 of her own money.

That's exactly what the intent of the Gold Award is: to acknowledge people

who give to the community through selfless acts.

Garcia plans to attend the University of Oregon next year _____
                                                         9. , / .

and she hopes to be a counselor someday _____ or a teacher of special
                                        10. , / Ø

needs students.

As for her mother _____ Betty, she's proud of her daughter. "It was
                  11. ; / ,

a lot of work," she said. "I witnessed everything. I saw it all come together, and I'm

proud of her."

....
[4] **juggling** managing more than one task at a time like both school and work

Chapter 11: Commonly Confused Words

*Read the following selection from the **Daily Pilot** newspaper. Choose the correct commonly confused word from the list in Chapter 11. If necessary, use a dictionary to choose the correct answer for other commonly confused words that are not presented in Chapter 11.*

For Their Health

by Ashley Breeding

Laguna Beach has _____ own Jamie Oliver.[1]
1. its / it's

Azmin Ghahreman, a chef and the owner of Sapphire Laguna, started a local food

revolution long before "The Naked Chef"[2] was on television. Three years ago,

Ghahreman began visiting schools _____ educate
2. too / to

children about healthy foods and cooking.

A parent of three, Ghahreman _____ he was
3. said / told

inspired to give all children the tools they need to make wiser food choices to

ensure better health and a brighter future.

"Child obesity has become a huge problem," he said. "We've all got to

do our share in life to touch the community, and my contribution is to help

_____ children. _____ our
4. are / our   **5. They're / There**

future."

Ghahreman added that education is "the most important thing. Once they

have this, they will know how to make better choices."

The chef recently visited Top of the World Elementary to

_____ an eight-week cooking class for students in
6. learn / teach

....

[1] **Jamie Oliver** a celebrity chef who is frequently on television

[2] **"The Naked Chef"** Jamie Oliver's television show about cooking

third through fifth grades. He exposed them to an array[3] of cultural cuisines and obscure[4] vegetables, and he gave nutrition tips.

We explored foods from China, Japan, the Middle East, Spain, France—all over," he said. "I also _____ them how important it is
                                    7. said / told
to eat breakfast and healthy snacks each day."

The children had a chance to _____ crepes,
                                    8. do / make
pasta dishes, and chocolate. They also learned about earth friendliness, kitchen cleanliness, and table etiquette.

"Many rules of life can be taught in the kitchen," said Ghahreman. "The kids really loved it and _____ a lot from it."
                                    9. brought / took

His hope, he said, is that kids will begin to demand more nutritious food from _____ parents and might even
                    10. their / there
_____ cooking as a family activity as he has with his
    11. adapt / adopt
own children.

"We want to give them the best—clothes, cars, Ivy League schools.[5] We must invest in their health, because _____ the foundation
                                    12. it's / its
for the rest of these things and their future," said the Iran-born chef who has travelled the world cooking in many countries.

....
[3] **array** a large group of things

[4] **obscure** not common or usual

[5] **Ivy League schools** schools in the United States that are considered the best

APPENDIX 2: IRREGULAR VERBS

Base Form	Simple Past	Past Participle
awake	awoke	awoken
be	was, were	been
beat	beat	beaten/beat
become	became	become
begin	began	begun
bend	bent	bent
bet	bet	bet
bind	bound	bound
bite	bit	bitten
bleed	bled	bled
blow	blew	blown
break	broke	broken
bring	brought	brought
broadcast	broadcast	broadcast
build	built	built
burn	burned	burned
buy	bought	bought
catch	caught	caught
choose	chose	chosen
cling	clung	clung
come	came	come
cost	cost	cost
creep	crept	crept
cut	cut	cut
deal	dealt	dealt
dig	dug	dug
dive	dove/dived	dived
do	did	done
draw	drew	drawn
dream	dreamed/dreamt	dreamed/dreamt
drink	drank	drunk
eat	ate	eaten
fall	fell	fallen
feed	fed	fed
feel	felt	felt
fight	fought	fought

Base Form	Simple Past	Past Participle
find	found	found
fit	fit	fit
flee	fled	fled
fly	flew	flown
forbid	forbade	forbidden
forecast	forecast	forecast
forget	forgot	forgotten
forgive	forgave	forgiven
freeze	froze	frozen
get	got	gotten
give	gave	given
go	went	gone
grind	ground	ground
grow	grew	grown
hang	hung	hung
have	had	had
hear	heard	heard
hide	hid	hidden
hit	hit	hit
hold	held	held
hurt	hurt	hurt
keep	kept	kept
know	knew	known
lay	laid	laid
lead	led	led
leave	left	left
lend	lent	lent
let	let	let
lie	lay	lain
light	lit/lighted	lit/lighted
lose	lost	lost
make	made	made
mean	meant	meant
meet	met	met
mislead	misled	misled
mistake	mistook	mistaken

Base Form	Simple Past	Past Participle	Base Form	Simple Past	Past Participle
misunderstand	misunderstood	misunderstood	split	split	split
overcome	overcame	overcome	spread	spread	spread
pay	paid	paid	spring	sprang	sprung
prove	proved	proven/proved	stand	stood	stood
put	put	put	steal	stole	stolen
quit	quit	quit	stick	stuck	stuck
read	read	read	sting	stung	stung
rid	rid	rid	stink	stank/stunk	stunk
ride	rode	ridden	strike	struck	struck/stricken
ring	rang	rung	string	strung	strung
rise	rose	risen	strive	strove/strived	striven
run	ran	run	swear	swore	sworn
say	said	said	sweep	swept	swept
see	saw	seen	swim	swam	swum
seek	sought	sought	swing	swung	swung
sell	sold	sold	take	took	taken
send	sent	sent	teach	taught	taught
set	set	set	tear	tore	torn
sew	sewed	sewn/sewed	tell	told	told
shake	shook	shaken	think	thought	thought
shed	shed	shed	throw	threw	thrown
shine	shone/shined	shone/shined	understand	understood	understood
shoot	shot	shot	undertake	undertook	undertaken
show	showed	shown	undo	undid	undone
shrink	shrank/shrunk	shrunk/shrunken	uphold	upheld	upheld
shut	shut	shut	upset	upset	upset
sing	sang	sung	wake	woke	woken/waked
sit	sat	sat	wear	wore	worn
sleep	slept	slept	weave	wove	woven
slide	slid	slid	weep	wept	wept
speak	spoke	spoken	wet	wet	wet
speed	sped/speeded	sped/speeded	win	won	won
spend	spent	spent	wind	wound	wound
spin	spun	spun	withdraw	withdrew	withdrawn
spit	spit/spat	spat	write	wrote	written

APPENDIX 3: SPELLING, CAPITALIZATION, AND APOSTROPHE RULES

This appendix gives you spelling rules, which can assist you in becoming a good speller. It also gives you rules for using apostrophes and for capitalization—two areas related to spelling. Keep this list handy so that you can refer to it while writing.

Spelling Rules for Words with *ie*

This rhyme gives the rule for using *i* and *e*

Use *i* before *e*

Except after *c*

Or when sounding like *a*

As in n*ei*ghbor and w*ei*gh.

Words with *ie*

| bel*ie*ve | ch*ie*f | f*ie*ld | gr*ie*f |

Words with *ei* after *c*

| rec*ei*ve | rec*ei*pt | c*ei*ling | dec*ei*t |

Words with *ei* sounding like *a*

| fr*ei*ght | v*ei*n | r*ei*gn | n*ei*ghbor |

Exceptions:

| *ei*ther | n*ei*ther | l*ei*sure | s*ei*ze |
| w*ei*rd | h*ei*ght | for*ei*gn | forf*ei*t |

Spelling Rules for Suffixes

- When adding *–ing* or another suffix that begins with a vowel or *–y*, drop the final silent *–e*.

    achieve + *–ing* — achiev*ing*

    locate + *–ion* — loca*tion*

    ice + *–y* — ic*y*

    Exceptions: change*able*   notice*able*   mile*age*   eye*ing*

- When adding *–ing*, change *–ie* to *–y*.

    die — d*ying*   tie — t*ying*   lie — l*ying*

- When adding a suffix that begins with a consonant, keep the final silent *–e*.

    discourage + *–ment* — discourage*ment*

    sincere + *–ly* — sincere*ly*

    Exceptions: argu*ment*   nin*th*   tru*ly*   who*lly*

- When a word ends in a consonant + *–y*, change *–y* to *–i* before adding a suffix.

    funny + *–er/–est*   — funn*ier*, funn*iest*

    try + *–ed* — tr*ied*

    allergy + *–ic* — allerg*ic*

    Do not make this change if the suffix is *–ing*: carry — carry*ing*

- When a word ends in a vowel + *–y*, keep the *–y*.

    delay — delay*ed*

- When a word has one syllable and ends in a single vowel + consonant, double the final consonant.

    pen — pen*ned*   big — big*ger*, big*gest*   sit — sit*ting*

- When a word has more than one syllable and ends in a single vowel + consonant, do not double the final consonant.

    happen — happen*ed*   focus — focus*ing*   commit — commit*ment*

Spelling Rules for Plurals

- When making most nouns plural, add –s.

  girl — girl*s*   radio — radio*s*
- When a noun ends in –ch, –sh, –s, or –x, add –es.

  church — church*es*   fox — fox*es*
- When a noun ends in a consonant + –o, add –es.

  potato — potato*es*   hero — hero*es*
- When a noun ends in a consonant + –y, drop the –y and add –ies.

  lady — lad*ies*   tragedy — traged*ies*

Spelling Rules for Prefixes

Add a prefix to the beginning of a word without doubling or dropping letters.

satisfy — *dis*satisfy   behave — *mis*behave   natural — *un*natural

Capitalization Rules

Rules for capitalization include the following:

1. Capitalize the first word of each sentence.
2. Capitalize proper nouns (nouns that name specific people, places, groups, and things, including languages and religious, ethnic, and political groups).

   John F. Kennedy, Vancouver, Spanish, Hispanic, Democrats
3. Capitalize adjectives of nationality and regional or religious affiliation.

   Brazilian restaurant, Basque region, Christian church
4. Capitalize titles before proper names.

   Professor William Su, Reverend Hoffman, Uncle Joe
5. Capitalize important words in titles of books, plays, movies, newspapers, magazines, and songs.

   Romeo and Juliet, The Sound of Music, The Daily Mirror, Newsweek
6. Capitalize historical events and periods.

   Korean War, the Cold War, Renaissance
7. Capitalize holidays, days, and months.

   Easter, Monday, January
8. Do not capitalize seasons.

   summer, spring, winter, fall/autumn

Apostrophe Rules

1. Use an apostrophe to show one or more letters have been left out.

   cannot — can't   that is — that's   we are — we're
2. Use an apostrophe to show ownership.

   the book of the student — the student's book

   the home of James — James's home or James' home

   the offices of the professors — the professors' offices

APPENDIX 4: PREPOSITIONS

Adjective + Preposition Combinations

This list contains some common adjective + preposition combinations. You can also check an ESL or learner's dictionary under the adjective for adjective + preposition combinations.

A
accustomed to
afraid of
amazed at/by
angry at
anxious about
ashamed of
aware of
awful at

B
bad at
bored with/by

C
capable of
concerned about
content with
curious about

D
dependent on
different from

E
eager for
envious of
excited about

F
familiar with
famous for
fond of
friendly to
full of

G
glad about
good at
guilty of

H
happy about
homesick for

I
inferior to
interested in

J
jealous of

K
known for

N
nervous
    about

O
opposed to

P
pleased about
proud of

R
ready for
responsible for

S
sad about
safe from
satisfied with
sick of
similar to
slow at
sorry for/about
suitable for
superior to
surprised about/at/by

T
terrible at
tired of

U
upset with

W
worried about

Verb + Preposition Combinations

This list contains common verb + preposition combinations. You can also check an ESL or learner's dictionary under the verb for verb + preposition combinations.

A
accuse someone of something
adapt to
admit to
advise against
agree with someone about something
apologize for
apply to/for
approve of
argue with someone about something
arrive at

B
believe in
belong to
blame someone for something

C
care about/for
choose between
combine something with
come from
compare someone/something to/with
complain to someone about something
concentrate on
consist of
contribute to
cooperate with
count on

D
deal with
decide on
depend on
disapprove of
dream about/of

E

escape from

excel at

excuse someone for

F

feel like

fight for

forget about

forgive someone for

G

glance at

gossip about

graduate from

H

happen to

hear about/of something

hear from someone

hide from

hope for

I

insist on

intend to

interfere with

introduce someone to someone

invite someone to something

K

know about

L

listen to

look at

look for

look forward to

learn from

live on

M

matter to

O

object to

P

participate in

pay for

plan on

prepare for

prevent someone/something from

profit from

protect someone/something from

prohibit someone from

R

read about

recover from

rely on

rescue from

respond to

S

search for

speak to/with someone about something

stare at

stop from

subscribe to

substitute for

succeed in

T

take advantage of

take care of

talk to/with someone about something

thank someone for something

think about/of

V

vote for

W

wait for

worry about

APPENDIX 5: CORRECTION SYMBOLS

Your teacher may use symbols to indicate specific error types in your writing. The charts below include symbols, explanations, and sample sentences for some of these errors. You can also use these symbols to help make the necessary corrections while you are editing your own work. Chart 1 refers to grammar items that are presented in Grammar for Writing 1. For further explanation and practice, refer to the indicated chapters. Chart 2 presents other common correction symbols.

CHART 1

SYMBOL	MEANING	SAMPLE SENTENCE	GRAMMAR FOR WRITING 1
cs	comma splice	It was a beautiful day, there wasn't a cloud in the sky.	Chapter 10
det	determiner error	It is a most interesting book I have read.	Chapter 7
frag	fragment	When we practice. The team must work together.	Chapter 10
num	noun error (number)	We have enough homeworks to last a week.	Chapter 6
p	punctuation error	I remember, graduation as the most memorable event.	Chapter 10
prn	pronoun error	My friend and me went to the movies.	Chapter 8
ref	unclear pronoun reference	We enjoyed the book and the movie but it was more violent.	Chapter 8
ro	run-on	The lecture was very interesting it went by so fast.	Chapter 10
s–v	subject–verb agreement error	She never go to the library to study.	Chapter 3
t	verb tense error	We haven't completed the project yesterday.	Chapters 1, 2, 4, 5
vb	verb form error	They haven't went to the gym in weeks.	Chapter 5, 9
wf	word form error	Her father is the most success software engineer in the firm.	Chapter 11
ww	wrong word	He is the best offensive player in the team.	Chapter 11

CHART 2

SYMBOL	MEANING	SAMPLE SENTENCE
sp	spelling error	sp My apartment is noisey and expensive.
^	insert missing word	in They are interested ^going with us to the concert.
ℰ	delete	ℰ His writing is clear, and concise, and interesting to read.
¶	paragraph	¶ This is the prominent theme. A secondary theme explains . . .
//	faulty parallelism	We hoped for relaxation, peace and to have good weather. //
#	add a space	# My friends went to the club eventhough it's very expensive.
(move here)	move here	The book was interesting that I stayed up all night reading.
(transpose)	transpose	We hardly could remember the way to your house.

APPENDIX 6: EDITING LOG

Use this editing log or create a similar one of your own to keep track of the grammar errors that you make in your writing. By logging and correcting your errors, you will begin to see which errors you make the most. Once you recognize the grammar items that are the most problematic for you, editing becomes easier.

ERROR	SYMBOL	ORIGINAL SENTENCE	REVISED SENTENCE
Subject-verb agreement	s-v	The essays I wrote about Chinese history was the best in the class.	The essays I wrote about Chinese history were the best in the class.

APPENDIX 7: GRAMMAR BOOK REFERENCES

GRAMMAR FOR WRITING 1	BASIC ENGLISH GRAMMAR, THIRD EDITION	FUNDAMENTALS OF ENGLISH GRAMMAR, FOURTH EDITION	FOCUS ON GRAMMAR 3, FOURTH EDITION
Chapter 1 Expressing Present Time	Chapter 1 Using *Be*, 1–2, 1–5, 1–8, Chapter 2 Using *Be* and *Have*, 2–1, 2–2, 2–3, 2–4, 2–8 Chapter 3 Using the Simple Present Chapter 4 Using the Present Progressive Chapter 9 Expressing Past Time, Part 2, 9–9 Chapter 10 Expressing Future Time, Part 1, 10–5	Chapter 1 Present Time Chapter 4 Present Perfect and Past Perfect: 4–1, 4–2, 4–3, 4–4, 4–5	Unit 1 Present Progressive and Simple Present Unit 8 Present Perfect: *Since* and *For* Unit 9 Present Perfect: *Already*, *Yet*, and *Still* Unit 10 Present Perfect: Indefinite Past Appendix 2 Non-action Verbs
Chapter 2 Expressing Past Time	Chapter 8 Expressing Past Time, Part 1 Chapter 9 Expressing Past Time, Part 2 Chapter 10 Expressing Future Time, Part 1, 10–3, 10–4, 10–5	Chapter 2 Past Time Chapter 4 Present Perfect and Past Perfect: 4–8 Appendix A-1 The Present Perfect vs. The Past Perfect Appendix A-2 The Past Progressive vs. The Past Perfect	Unit 2 Simple Past Unit 3 Past Progressive and Simple Past Unit 4 *Used to* and *Would* Unit 11 Present Perfect and Simple Past Part I From Grammar to Writing: Combining Sentences with Time Words
Chapter 3 Subject-Verb Agreement	Chapter 1 Using *Be*: 1–3, Chapter 2 Using *Be* and *Have*: 2–4 Chapter 3 Using the Simple Present: 3–1, 3–7, 3–9, 3–10 Chapter 4 Using the Present Progressive: 4–1, 4–3, 4–4 Chapter 14 Nouns and Modifiers: 14–4	Chapter 1 Present Time: 1–2 Chapter 2 Past Time: 2–1, 2–6 Chapter 3 Future Time: 3–2, 3–3 Chapter 6 Nouns and Pronouns, 6–7	Unit 1 Present Progressive and Simple Present Unit 2 Simple Past Unit 3 Past Progressive and Simple Past Unit 8 Present Perfect: Since and For
Chapter 4 Expressing Future Time	Chapter 10 Expressing Future Time, Part 1	Chapter 3 Future Time	Unit 6 The Future Unit 7 Future Time Clauses
Chapter 5 Time Shifts and Tenses	See references for Chapters 1–4	See references for Chapters 1–4	See references for Chapters 1–4
Chapter 6 Count and Uncountable Nouns	Chapter 7 Count and Noncount Nouns	Chapter 11 Count/Noncount Nouns and Articles: 11–2, 11–3, 11–4, 11–5, 11–6, 11–7	Unit 17 Nouns and Quantifiers Unit 18: Articles: Indefinite and Definite Appendix 7 Non-count Nouns
Chapter 7 Articles and Other Determiners	Chapter 1 Using *Be*: 1–1, 1–2 Chapter 2 Using *Be* and *Have*: 2–5, 2–6, 2–7 Chapter 7 Count and Noncount Nouns: 7–1, 7–2, 7–3, 7–5, 7–6, 7–7, 7–8	Chapter 11 Count/Noncount Nouns and Articles: 11–1, 11–8, 11–9	Unit 18: Articles: Indefinite and Definite

GRAMMAR FOR WRITING 1	BASIC ENGLISH GRAMMAR, THIRD EDITION	FUNDAMENTALS OF ENGLISH GRAMMAR, FOURTH EDITION	FOCUS ON GRAMMAR 3, FOURTH EDITION
Chapter 8 and Pronouns	Chapter 1 Using *Be*: 1–3 Chapter 6 Nouns and Pronouns: 6–3 Chapter 14 Indefinite Pronouns: 14–6, 14–7 Chapter 15 Possessives: 15–3	Chapter 6 Nouns and Pronouns: 6–10, 6–12, 6–13, 6–14, 6–15, 6–16	Unit 27 Reflexive and Reciprocal Pronouns Part VIII From Grammar to Writing: Using Pronouns for Coherence
Chapter 9 Modals	Chapter 11 Expressing Future Time, Part 2: 11–1 Chapter 12 Modals, Part 1: Expressing Ability Chapter 13 Modals, Part 2: Advice, Necessity, Requests, Suggestions	Chapter 7 Modal Auxiliaries Chapter 10 The Passive: 10–5	Unit 13 Ability: *Can, Could, Be able to* Unit 14 Permission: *Can, Could, May, Do you mind if* Unit 15 Requests: *Can, Could, Will, Would, Would you mind* Unit 16 Advice: *Should, Ought to, Had better* Unit 29 Necessity: *Have (got) to, Must, Don't have to, Must not, Can't* Unit 30 Expectations: *Be supposed to* Unit 31 Future Possibility: *May, Might, Could* Unit 32 Conclusions: *Must, Have (got) to, May, Might, Could, Can't* Part IV From Grammar to Writing: Using Appropriate Modals Appendix 19 Modals and Their Functions
Chapter 10 Sentence Structure and Punctuation	Chapter 2 Using *Be* and *Have*, 2–1 Chapter 9 Expressing Past Time, Part 2: 9–7, 9–10 Chapter 11 Expressing Future Time, Part 2: 11–3 Chapter 16 Making Comparisons: 16–6	Chapter 2 Past Time: 2–7 Chapter 8 Connecting Ideas: 8–1, 8–2, 8–3, 8–6, 8–7 Chapter 11 Count/Noncount Nouns and Articles: 11–10 Chapter 14 Noun Clauses: 14–7	Part VII From Grammar to Writing: Combining Sentences with *and, but, so, or* Part IX From Grammar to Writing: Combining Sentences with *because, although, even though* Appendix 27 Capitalization and Punctuation Rules
Chapter 11 Commonly Confused Words	-	-	-

APPENDIX 8: ACADEMIC WORD LIST

The Academic Word List was developed in 2000 by Averil Coxhead from a written academic corpus of material used in the fields of liberal arts, commerce, law, and science. It contains 570 words that appear most frequently in this corpus.

Chapter 1
academic
academically
community
culture
cultures
decades
defines
errors
finance
focus
goal
grades
individual
involvement
located
location
normally
positive
stress
traditional

Chapter 2
anticipated
area
communicate
economy
finally
grade
ignore
ignored
job
mature
partner
promoted
promotion
region
role

Chapter 3
adult
area
areas
available
benefits

communicate
communicates
community
computers
draft
editor
final
finally
flexibility
grades
job
process
require
residential
revise
revising
revision
revisions
style
styles
techniques
transfer

Chapter 4
administrative
assistants
computers
construction
final
finally
grade
job
lecture
lectures
predict
resources
technology
traditional

Chapter 5
adapting
appropriate
approximately
area
challenges

commission
computer
environment
migration
normal
significantly
traditional

Chapter 6
areas
assigned
computers
decades
environment
environmental
finally
generations
global
grade
guarantees
sources

Chapter 7
academic
achieved
assistance
benefits
communication
cultural
diversity
energy
environment
grades
injuries
instructors
job
location
medium
method
motivate
motivated
motivating
motivation
negative
overseas

positive
reinforcement
resources
style
unique
whereas

Chapter 8
accurate
adults
alternative
benefit
commit
committing
communities
community
contribute
culture
cultures
definitely
diversity
ethical
ethnic
finally
generation
illegal
immigrant
immigrants
individuality
minor
professional
require
required
theories
theory
traditions
violations

Chapter 9
adulthood
adults
create
culture
environmental
final

CREDITS

Photos

Pages 2, 15, 26, 33, 41, 48, 55, 82: Shutterstock.com; **Page 65:** blphoto/Alamy; **Page 92:** iStockphoto.com.

Text

Pages 107–108: "Triple Threat" by Scott Barajas. OC Register. Reprinted with permission; **Pages 109–110:** "Students Set up Outdoor Library" by Carla Rivera. Copyright © 2010 Los Angeles Times. Reprinted with Permission; **Pages 111–112:** "A Very Able Crew" by Torence Loose. Coast Magazine, May 1999. Reprinted with permission; **Pages 113–114:** "Arts in the Real World" by Tina Sustarsic and Michaela Baltasar. New University Newspaper 5/29/2000. Reprinted with permission; **Pages 115–116:** "Stand Up Sport" by Brian Lichterman. The Independent, June 11, 2010. Reprinted with the permission of Newport Beach Independent, Published by Firebrand Media, LLC; **Pages 117:** "Dog Masters ESL" El Gazette New Media, March 2010. The original story is available at www.elgazettedigital.com. Reprinted with Permission; **Pages 118–119:** "A Good Impression" by Jennifer Garrison. Copyright © 2010. Daily Pilot. Reprinted with Permission; **Pages 120–121:** "Giving back the gift" by Carroll Lachnit Reprinted with Permission of Orange Coast Magazine; **Pages 122–123:** "This Time, Interviewer is in Spotlight" by Stephanie Sheh, 2/19/1999. Student Media UCLA. Reprinted with permission; **Pages 124–125:** "Worth the Right Word" by Tom Ragen. Copyright © 2010. Daily Pilot. Reprinted with permission; **Pages 126–127:** "For their health" written by Ashley Breeding. Copyright © 2010. Daily Pilot. Reprinted with Permission.